The Business System
A Bicentennial View

The Business System
A Bicentennial View

Milton Friedman
Leonard S. Silk
Pehr G. Gyllenhammar
Eli Ginzberg
Edward E. David, Jr.
William D. Carey
John W. Hennessey, Jr.

With an Introduction by
Frederick E. Webster, Jr.

PUBLISHED BY THE AMOS TUCK SCHOOL OF
BUSINESS ADMINISTRATION

DISTRIBUTED BY THE UNIVERSITY PRESS
OF NEW ENGLAND
HANOVER NEW HAMPSHIRE 1977

CONTENTS

ILLUSTRATIONS

INTRODUCTION

THE SEVENTY-FIFTH ANNIVERSARY of the Amos Tuck School of Business Administration came during the bicentennial year of the United States of America. From this coincidence was forged the theme of Tuck's diamond anniversary celebration— *The Business System: A Bicentennial View.* It was felt that Tuck could more than justify this hitchhiking on the bicentennial theme because education for professional management was an American invention and Tuck was America's first graduate school of business administration.

Moreover, 1976 was also the bicentennial year of the publication of Adam Smith's famous treatise *An Inquiry into the Nature and Causes of the Wealth of Nations.* It would be hard to cite another work of greater relevance to the study of the free enterprise system and management within that system, or a work that has proven more timeless. Thus many of the speakers in this symposium found it useful to refer to Adam Smith's great work.

From this confluence of the anniversaries of the founding of the Tuck School, the birth of the American nation, and the publication of *The Wealth of Nations* emerged the three session themes around which the Symposium was organized:

Economics and Social Progress: Adam Smith Plus Two Hundred Years

Modern Institutions and Individual Freedom: Thomas Jefferson Plus Two Hundred Years

Technology for Man: Benjamin Franklin Plus Two Hundred Years

The symposium was planned to be an inquiry, a stock-taking, a looking backward and ahead, not a presentation of the state of the art in such familiar fields as finance, organizational behavior, and marketing. It was to be an attempt to define and discuss some of the most serious issues facing the business society, such as worker alienation, imperfections in the market system, the appropriate uses of technology, and the potential conflict between the growth of bureaucracy and individual freedom.

Some observers, if constrained by a parochial view of the appropriate concerns of a school of management, might regard these themes as too broad, but those who founded the Tuck School would surely have approved. When President Edward Tucker wrote from Paris in 1899 to Professors Colby and Wells, telling them that the original Tuck gift was in the offing, he asked them to begin preparations for establishing a "School of Political Economy and Finance." Among the subjects taught at Tuck at the beginning of the century were social statistics, European political history, anthropological geography, demography, social institutions, international trade relations, diplomacy, and a history of American industrial development, as well as such basic fare as economics, money and banking, public finance, and transportation.

In his remarks to the anniversary banquet gathering on the last evening of the celebration, John Hennessey, ending his term as the fifth dean of the Tuck School, spoke of the personal relationship between Mr. Edward Tuck and Dartmouth's President Tucker, who were college roommates during their Dartmouth undergraduate years. As so often happens, a great personal friendship became the basis for an institutional innovation of great social consequence. When the Dartmouth trustees voted on January 19, 1900, to create the Amos Tuck School of Business Administration, they created a precedent that would one day be followed by most of the great universities of the United States.

The Original Tuck Hall, now McNutt Hall.

The shape of the Tuck School, like that of any viable, responsive institution, has continually evolved in a fashion determined by its accomplishments, problems, resources, and opportunities. From the early days when the undergraduate program at Dartmouth was the only source of students, Tuck has grown to a student body of 270 men and women drawn from over 90 undergraduate institutions in the United States and a dozen other countries. The early curricular emphasis on economics, finance, sociology, history, and political science has matured to include the sophistication of organizational behavior, computer science, multivariate statistics, multinational enterprise, management of technological change, and many other subjects reflecting the accomplishments, concerns, and complexity of the post-industrial or "affluent" society.

A visible record of this evolutionary progress is seen in the architectural changes from Tuck's early home in what was then

Tuck Hall, Flanked by Chase Hall and Woodbury Hall.

Tuck Hall (now McNutt Hall), built in 1904 with funds provided by Mr. Tuck, to the new Tuck Hall in 1930, and finally to the magnificent facilities of the Murdough Center, including Feldberg Library, Bosworth Computation Center, the Ankeny, Barclay, and Stoneman classrooms, and Cook Auditorium, completed in 1973.

Throughout its seventy-five year history, Tuck has maintained its original emphasis upon preparing young people for *general* management responsibilities. Newspaper reports of the founding of the school in 1900 referred to "The Amos Tuck School of Actual Affairs" and noted:

The Dartmouth authorities realized that a graduate school should not and could not be a commercial college; that it must present not so much details as principles; and that these principles must be based not only on the general culture of a college education, but on a special study of finance, economics, history, law, and politics. They realized that the young man leaving such a school must be prepared, not for mere clerkship—which was a matter of practical training—but for a position of responsibility and control, and knowing that in such a position a man's outlook must be of the widest, they made up the two years' course which was begun in September with the formal opening of the new school.

President Tucker's vision, shared with Mr. Tuck, was one of preparing young people (only men in those days) for business *leadership,* not just careers. As Dean Hennessey noted in his speech, raising business leadership to the dignity of a profession required not only teaching knowledge, skills, and attitudes but, most fundamentally, instilling in future leaders a sense of obligation to one's fellow man.

The leadership posture of Tuck in this regard has been reasserted in a number of ways. For example, Professor Wayne G. Broehl developed a course in Business and Society in the 1950's that has been a model for many other schools. This course, which has now evolved into the Business Environments course at Tuck, raised issues of business ethics and corporate responsibility against a background of business history and in the context of such specific problems as the role of the board of directors, equal employment opportunity, and corporate philanthropy.

Tuck's continuing dedication to the task of preparing students for general management and professional leadership responsibilities is confirmed in another way. Not only was Tuck the first graduate school of management, but it remains the only school in the United States, among more than 190 accredited collegiate business schools, to offer *only* the master's degree. All others combine either undergraduate or doctoral education, or both, with their master's degree programs. Tuck's strategy commits its full resources to what it can do best—professional education for management responsibilities.

The Murdough Center.

The symposium, "The Business System: A Bicentennial View," thus has a tone that reflects the historical and strategic uniqueness of the Amos Tuck School. It is not an inward-looking recollecting of accomplishments but an outward-looking assessment of some of the major issues facing management of large complex organizations, private and public, in a troubled interdependent world. Many of these issues involve the interface of business and government and the interaction of the individual with formal organization. At the deepest level, whether the subject is the functioning of the market economy, organization, or technology, a concern for humanistic values predominates. The lecturers speak often of individual freedom, not in a trivial or nationalistic tone but in the most profound sense of respect for the ultimate dignity of every man.

Given this tone and these common concerns, it was not surprising that the three symposium themes seemed to blend

Stoneman Classroom, One of Three Such Rooms in the Murdough Center.

and merge in all sessions. The flow of ideas was as broadly
sweeping as had been hoped for; differing viewpoints added up
to a whole perspective that was more than the sum of its parts.
It was inevitable that the attractive opportunity to hark back to
Adam Smith would appeal to virtually all of the speakers, not
just those commenting on "Economics and Social Progress."
From these differing viewpoints emerges a perspective on Smith
that is not just balanced but also richer and, even more, testimony to the depth and quality of his thinking. As several speakers demonstrate, Smith's comments have as much relevance
today as they did in 1776, despite the greater complexity of our
problems.

Professor Milton Friedman, who was awarded the Nobel
Prize in Economic Science later in 1976, asks whether the past
two hundred years had indeed represented social progress, and
calls for the reassertion of the basic values of the free enterprise

system. A different tone is set by Dr. Leonard Silk as he observes that "events of the nineteenth and twentieth centuries have demonstrated that the existence of markets is no guarantee against the breakdown of economic systems and no safeguard against political tyranny." Professor Friedman would certainly disagree with Dr. Silk's defense of modifications of the free enterprise system "to make it more humane, to protect it from excesses of market power, to preserve basic liberties." But from this coming together of opposing viewpoints emerges a realization that the most important questions of economic science are those of issues, values, and philosophy, not those of method and technique. Furthermore, we develop new awareness that moral issues are never simple, and new wariness of those who propose simple answers to those issues.

Although the next session on "Modern Institutions and Individual Freedom" was subtitled "Thomas Jefferson Plus Two Hundred Years," in reference to Jefferson's basically democratic views and respect for the individual's ability to define his own best interest, Mr. Pehr Gustav Gyllenhammar also quoted Adam Smith in his opening words: "A worker gives up his ease, his liberty, and his happiness when he goes into industry." Mr. Gyllenhammar says this is only a slight exaggeration and is still basically true, then proceeds to describe steps he has encouraged at Volvo to redesign the work environment, beginning with fundamental production technology. Volvo has attacked problems of worker alienation, turnover, and product quality by scrapping the traditional assembly line in favor of a work group form of organization. As this Scandinavian business statesman describes these changes, it becomes clear that there are two inseparable sets of objectives and motivations. One set is concerned with economic considerations of labor cost, production efficiency, and product quality. The other set is concerned with finding solutions to a social problem which have the potential to benefit industry and society at large. It is refreshing to hear a

Feldberg Library, in Murdough.

manager who believes that corporate welfare and social welfare cannot be separated for very long.

Dr. Eli Ginzberg, whose amazingly productive career as a scholar began with a dissertation entitled "The House of Adam Smith," also elected to build his themes around *The Wealth of Nations.* Making extensive use of quotations from Smith, Dr. Ginzberg shows that Smith was a management theorist as well as an economist. He comments upon the role of the individual worker, the work environment, and the division of labor, as well as Smith's views concerning American independence.

In his introduction to the session on "Technology for Man," Professor J. Brian Quinn commented upon the dual nature of technology as handmaiden of mankind and evil genie. He phrases the concerns of the session as a series of provocative questions, among them:

—Are existing institutions capable of directing science and technology for the benefit of humanity?

—What new incentives are necessary to obtain a humanistic response to the opportunities and threats posed by technology?

—Does technological progress necessarily mean new incursions on freedom?

—Must technology lead to large bureaucratic institutions with their side effects of alienation and anxiety?

Dr. Edward E. David, Jr., notes his own sense of encouragement at the new concern for value issues in technology and the recognition that "technology does not always take us where we want to go." But he also sees another issue emerging—the threat that technology assessment will become technology arrestment. Once again Adam Smith's "invisible hand" appears, as David asks whether it is possible for government to play its role in technology assessment and advancement "without stifling the spontaneity of the cohort of diverse contributors who have traditionally determined the future through their thousands of personal decisions and personal interests pursued day after day." How much can government supplement and compliment market forces without destroying the incentives and protections of the market system?

Along similar lines, the next speaker, Mr. William Carey, refers to Hazel Henderson's concept of the Entropy State, where the complexity of bureaucratic checks, balances, and countermeasures reaches such excessive levels that society slowly winds down as it reaches a balanced state of equilibrium. Mr. Carey, who has had a distinguished career in public services, raises some basic issues about the appropriate uses of government and worries aloud, deeply and movingly, about an antigovernment psychology in America: "If we run the public service down, if we hound it, if we show only contempt for it, then we will break its heart and its spirit, and I call that wrong. We will get a third-rate public service if our expectations for it are third-rate. We will drive off the best of our young people from public service as a career, and we will end with what we deserve." More generally, Mr. Carey senses a pervasive negativism toward all social institutions and technology. He rejects the proposition that quality of life and technology are incompatible.

In addition, Mr. Carey asks some disturbing questions about the lack of accountability of organizations that are not wholly in either the public or the private sectors, accountable neither to the political process nor to the forces of the marketplace. As organized social-political activity increasingly becomes dominated by voluntaristic, idealistic "third-sector" or "quasi-nongovernmental" organizations, there is indeed cause for concern.

The symposium speakers define and discuss some vitally important issues facing management in the two hundredth year of the nation. The present volume is intended to serve a dual purpose. First, it is a record of the symposium itself, the issues and the ideas that were debated. We hope that the debate will continue in other places, stimulated by these papers. Second, they are, as the symposium was, a brief celebration of the unique history of the Amos Tuck School of Business Administration and an updated reassertion of the basic values and deep concerns that led to its founding seventy-five years ago.

January 1977   *Frederick E. Webster, Jr.*
                                  Associate Dean
                                  Chairman of the Symposium

Part One
Economics and Social Progress:
Adam Smith Plus Two Hundred Years

1. THE INVISIBLE HAND

Milton Friedman

Milton Friedman is Paul Snowden Russell Distinguished Ser-vice Professor of Economics at the University of Chicago, a member of the research staff of the National Bureau of Economic Research, and a columnist and contributing editor for News-week. *He has held several visiting professorships in the United States and at Cambridge University and served in a variety of research and teaching posts before joining the Chicago faculty. Among his many publications are eighteen books. He was elected to the National Academy of Science in 1973 and was awarded the Nobel Prize in 1976.*

I HEAR talk of the progress of the business system in the past two hundred years, as if there had been continuous progress. There has not been. There has been progress and there has been retrogress. There have been areas in which the progress has been met, so that we stand today in a very much better position than we did two hundred years ago. But in other respects we have returned to the state of affairs as it was in Great Britain at the time when Adam Smith wrote his first great work, *The Wealth of Nations.*

There is a great misunderstanding about Adam Smith, a serious misconception of his role. Because he is known as the father of laissez-faire, because of his emphasis on the "invisible hand," and because he explained the virtues of the price system, Smith is ordinarily regarded as if he were a defender of the status quo, a representative of the existing institutions, part of the establishment. He was anything but that. Smith was a revolu-

Dr. Milton Friedman.

tionary, one of a small minority who attacked the existing order
of things. At the time he wrote in the late eighteenth century,
Britain was a mercantilist state, in which the government was
exercising almost as great a control over economic affairs as the
United States government does now. It was a state of affairs in
which there were restrictions on imports and exports, there were
remnants of the guild system of the middle ages, and so on down
the line. Adam Smith attacked this system. His book was a tract

for reform, calling for a revolution in the way in which economic affairs were conducted. Smith, who was not a naive man, did not expect to succeed. "To expect indeed," he said, "that the freedom of trade should ever to entirely restored in Great Britain, is as absurd as to expect that an Oceania or a Utopia should ever be established in it. Not only the prejudices of the public, but what is much more unconquerable, the private interests of many individuals, irresistibly oppose it." Those are precisely my sentiments today.

Business enterprises are, in fact, a main obstacle to a restoration of freedom of trade. Every business enterprise claims a belief in Adam Smith's principles for everybody else, but not for itself. The steel industry, or the U.S. Steel Corporation, takes out full-page ads to tell you how great a system free enterprise is. It also sends its lobbyists to Washington to foster tariffs and import quotas on steel. The oil companies sing hymns of praise to the free enterprise system, but only a few years back they were in the forefront of those supporting import quotas on oil and in favor of the prorationing of oil in Texas and Oklahoma. Business enterprises do not promote and foster freedom of trade today any more than they did in Adam Smith's day. It was precisely that which Smith was referring to when he said that not only the prejudices of the public, but the private interests of many irresistibly oppose it.

The interesting thing is that Smith was wrong. He said that it was absurd to expect free trade to be established, yet free trade *was* established, though not for some seventy years after his great book appeared. It came out in 1776, and the basic step that dismantled the trade barriers and brought back free trade in Britain—namely, the repeal of the corn laws—took place in 1846. That was when free trade was established in Great Britain. In the United States a reasonable approximation to freedom of enterprise prevailed through most of the nineteenth century but not fundamentally on grounds of principle. Alexander Hamilton, our first Secretary of the Treasury and author of *The Report on the Manufacturers,* quoted or paraphrased Smith in that report in a number of places, but mostly to refute him—or, more accurately, to try to do so. He ended with proposals that Smith would have rejected out of hand. Hamilton proposed a tariff system, a system of protection for domestic industry, strictly contrary to the whole message of *The Wealth of Nations.*

Although the United States did have elements of protection throughout the nineteenth century—at least by comparison with the situation in Britain when Smith wrote, or as it is today in the United States—the United States had nearly complete freedom of trade at that time. The role of government was relatively small throughout the century. Except for the Civil War, total government spending in the United States never exceeded 10 percent of the national income, and two-thirds of that was state and local spending. Spending by the federal government never exceeded 3 percent of the national income, and most of that was for military expenditures. The major source of revenue was the tariff, which was in large part a revenue tariff, though to some extent it was also a protective tariff.

The situation is very different today. We are now drifting away—or, it would be more accurate to say, rushing away—from laissez-faire and free enterprise and toward collectivism. We have, I maintain, come full circle with respect to policy. Government plays a nearly dominant role in the economy. Total government spending has reached 40 percent of the national income, and two-thirds of it is federal. There is hardly an action that a business enterprise can undertake which does not require the approval or the oversight of one or another of those masses of bureaucrats who check on our every activity.

If Smith was wrong in his time in believing that free trade could not be restored, perhaps what today appears to be an almost impossible job of restoring it will turn out to be possible. Perhaps history *can* repeat itself, and, just as in Britain a popular crusade swept away the corn laws and the other restrictions on trade, so I would not rule out the possibility that in the United States a popular crusade, a revolt against big government, a revolt against bureaucracy, a revolt against heavy taxes could sweep away the interferences with free trade.

In judging that possibility and in analyzing our present state, what Adam Smith had to say two hundred years ago is as pertinent to our problems today as it was to the problems about which he talked. Let me suggest examples.

Consider a comment by Smith which could be applied to our national primaries, "That insidious and crafty animal, vulgarly called a statesman or politician, whose councils are directed by the momentary fluctuations of affairs." Or consider what he might have said about the Humphrey-Hawkins bill. That bill currently is a revised version of what was formerly the Humphrey-Javits bill and the Humphrey-Hawkins bill. It is supposed to bring central national planning to the country and to guarantee full employment. Here is what Adam Smith might have said about it: "The statesman, who should attempt to direct private people in what manner they ought to employ their capitals, would not only load himself with a most unnecessary attention, but assume an authority which could safely be trusted, not only to no single person but to no council or senate whatever, and which would nowhere be so dangerous as in the hands of a man who had folly and presumption enough to fancy himself fit to exercise it." A pretty accurate description of Mr. Humphrey, isn't it?

Or consider Smith's comment on the effect of growth of government intervention. In his time it took forms different from ours, but if he were making these comments today, he would surely have in mind the growth of the Interstate Commerce Commission, the Federal Communications Commission, the Federal Trade Commission, Amtrak, Conrail, and so on. Here is what he said: "Though the profusion of government must, undoubtedly, have retarded the natural progress of England toward wealth and improvement, it has not been able to stop it." Also, "The uniform, constant, and uninterrupted effort of every man to better his condition, the principle from which public and national, as well as private opulence is originally derived, is frequently powerful enough to maintain the natural progress of things toward improvement, in spite both of the extravagance of government and of the greatest errors of administration."

That seems a particularly pertinent comment. The fundamental question of this Tuck School conference is whether we have made progress because of interventions like the ICC and FCC or despite them. I share Smith's view that progress has clearly been despite and not because.

Let me suggest what Smith might have said about Ralph Nader or John Kenneth Galbraith and consumer protection laws: "It is the highest impertinence and presumption in kings and ministers, to pretend to watch over the economy of private people, and to restrain their expense, either by sumptuary laws, or by prohibiting the importation of foreign luxuries. They are themselves always, and without any exception, the greatest spendthrifts in the society. Let them look well after their own expense, and they may safely trust private people with theirs. If their own extravagance does not ruin the state, that of their subjects never will." Even Wayne Hayes could read that with profit.

Or consider another subject that is particularly relevant to the Tuck School. Students of Tuck have been heavily burdened with the question of social responsibility of corporations. Adam Smith had a succinct and pithy comment: "I have never known much good done by those who affected the trade for the public good." Or consider Smith's comment on taxes: "There is no art which one government sooner learns of another, than that of draining money from the pockets of people."

The great achievement of Adam Smith, which I think is over and beyond these wise comments on particular areas, the achievement that establishes *The Wealth of Nations* as the beginning of scientific economics, was his recognition of the "invisible hand"—of the way in which voluntary acts of millions of individuals each pursuing his own objectives could be coordinated, without central direction, through a price system. Let me quote his great key passage:

As every individual, therefore, endeavors as much as he can both to employ his capital in the support of domestic industry, and so to direct that industry that its produce be of the greatest value; every individual necessarily labors to render the annual revenue of the society as great as he can. He generally, indeed, neither intends to promote the public interest, nor knows how much he is promoting it. He intends only his own gain, and he is in this, as in many other cases, led by an invisible hand to promote an end which was no part of his intention. Nor is it always the worse for the society that it was no part of it. By pursuing his own interest he frequently promotes that of the society more effectually than when he really intends to promote it.

I submit that that's an extremely sophisticated and subtle insight. As we look about the world, what looks like chaos at first sight is, Smith points out, a system. Here somehow or other are millions of people all over the world cooperating, people who do not know one another, who have never heard of one another, who do not speak the same language, yet they are cooperating without being told to do so, and without central direction. Every day we are using in one way or another the output of people in faraway lands.

Leonard Read in a talk once used the marvelous example of a lead pencil: "You know, it's a funny thing, nobody knows how to make a pencil." He is right. In order to make a pencil you have to have wood; in order to have wood you have to cut down trees; to cut down trees you have to have saws; to get saws you have to make steel; to get steel you have to mine the ore, build blast furnaces, and so on. In a single pencil somehow or other is incorporated all of that knowledge and activity, and more besides. The graphite that is the center of it comes from mines in South America or somewhere. I do not know exactly where. The red rubber tip of the pencil probably came from Malaya. The rubber tree was not even native to Malaya, it was imported into Malaya from South America by individuals who were seeking only their own interest. How is it that people in Malaya know that they are supposed to produce rubber for you to use on that pencil? Where is the genius sitting in some central office sending orders to Malaya telling people, "produce a little bit of rubber for that pencil?" Somehow or other knowledge and abilities, scattered and diversified among millions of people and not accessible to a central intelligence or a central knowledge, are coordinated and organized by an impersonal price mechanism which nobody created, nobody invented, nobody deliberately organized.

The great and subtle insight of Smith, the "invisible hand," is the way in which the price system operates silently and invisibly. We do not see its external tracks. Yet it works. People are seldom aware of a complicated machine as long as it is working. Only when your car breaks down at three o'clock in the morning on a dark and lonely road do you realize what a complicated mechanism it is. Only when the price system breaks down because it is not permitted to operate—as has been the case in many places, most recently in Argentina—do we realize what a complex and delicate system it is.

The second reason why it is difficult for people to appreciate this great insight is that it is commonly believed that explicit reason and rationality are necessary in order for a system to be created. In many ways, the most difficult idea to grasp is that it is possible for a complex, interrelated system to develop and to function through the autonomous behavior of many

What Smith was pointing out then, and what is equally true now, is that sympathy is like gravitation: its strength decreases as the inverse square of the distance. We have far more sympathy for those close to us and dear to us than we can possibly have for those far away. That is why Smith saw little good to come from those who profess to trade for the public good.

The error of modern, well intentioned liberals, central planners of the Humphrey-Hawkins type, the error of those who seek to attack major social problems by the political mechanism, is brought out, I think, extremely well in my favorite quotation from Smith, again from *The Theory of Moral Sentiments*. Smith had a name for the kind of man you all are familiar with, who believes that society should be run by central direction, who believes that able, smart men should design a system for the rest of us, who believes that these men should sit in a central location with tentacles spread throughout the society, deciding social priorities and who should do what. He called such people "men of system," and this is what he had to say about them:

The man of system seems to imagine that he can arrange the different members of a great society with as much ease as the hand arranges the different pieces upon a chessboard; he does not consider that the pieces upon the chessboard have no other principle of motion besides that which the hand impresses upon them; but that, in the great chess-board of human society, every single piece has a principle of motion of its own, altogether different from that which the legislature might choose to impress upon it. If these two principles coincide and act in the same direction, the game of human society will go on easily and harmoniously, and is very likely to be happy and successful. If they are opposite or different, the game will go on miserably, and the society must be at all times in the highest degree of disorder.

Now that last sentence is not a bad description of the present. "Society must be at all times in the highest degree of disorder." Why? Because a man of system has tried to treat the individual citizen of a country as if he were a piece on a chessboard, instead of an autonomous human being with his own motives, his own urges, his own values. The failure to understand this central insight of Adam Smith is the reason why I believe that there is an invisible hand in politics as there is in economics, but one that works in the opposite direction. Adam Smith pointed out that in the economic market, the man who intends only his own good will tend to promote the good of society better than the man who intends to promote the good of society. In the political world, the invisible hand operates in the other way. The well meaning reformer who intends solely to promote the interest of society is led by an invisible hand to promote private interest that it was no part of his intention to promote. And he and his fellows produce in the process that "highest degree of disorder." That is, above all, the lesson Adam Smith has to teach.

2. MORAL ISSUES OF TODAY'S ECONOMICS

Leonard S. Silk

Leonard Silk is a member of the Editorial Board and a financial columnist for The New York Times. *Prior to joining* The Times *in 1970, he was a Senior Fellow at The Brookings Institution (1969), and had been with* Business Week *from 1954 to 1969, serving as Editorial Page Editor and Chairman of the Editorial Board from 1967. He earned a doctorate in economics at Duke University in 1947 and has held several distinguished academic appointments. He began his newspaper career as a reporter for* The Atlantic City Press, *and worked as a United States Army newspaper reporter and editor during World War II. He is the author of several books and has often been honored as a business journalist.*

EVERY GREAT AUTHOR runs the risk of being perverted and misused by his admirers and adulators. Plato, Machiavelli, Rousseau, Marx, Nietzsche, and Keynes have all suffered at the hand of their disciples from time to time. So has Adam Smith. His *Wealth of Nations* became the new Bible for the emerging capitalist class, and the industrial revolution was carried forward under its authority. Smithian principles of noninterference by government were used or abused to justify child labor, hazardous and harsh working conditions, low wages, long hours, wretched housing, and other evils associated with rapid industrialization. It is true, however, that to Smith such conditions did not seem as terrible as the abuses of freedom which stemmed from author-

Dr. Leonard S. Silk.

itarian governments and feudal masters. He was writing at a time
when the old structures of society were buckling under the strain
of new economic forces. He strongly believed that free enterprise
uninhibited by government was necessary to facilitate advances
in technology, to promote expansion of trade at home and
abroad, and to enable men to enjoy new political freedom. The
free market would also create new sources of wealth, he felt,
and the old landowning and, in some cases, sert- and slaveowning

class would gradually lose control of the tenants and retainers under them. This did indeed happen, although industrialism brought its own injustices and cruelties.

Smith, as Professor Friedman has said, was no Utopian. He did not believe that a free market and what came to be christened (by Marx) capitalism together provided the solution to every social problem. Always a careful observer, he was often his own best critic. He anticipated many of the injustices of the market which later economists would discover. He warned against the greed of the capitalists and their desire to monopolize and thereby remove the controls upon their prices and quality of goods by getting rid of competition. "People of the same trade," he said in a quotation that is almost as famous as the metaphor of the invisible hand, "seldom meet, whether for merriment or diversion, but the conversation ends in a conspiracy against the public or in some contrivance to raise prices." So in due course, in the two hundred years that I am to account for, came the antitrust laws, which I believe do not have ardent admirers at the University of Chicago.

Smith foresaw that division of labor among workers in factories would breed intense boredom and what Marx would later call alienation. He urged that the growth of industry be paralleled by a growth in education to keep the worker who spent his whole day repeating one operation from being turned into a brute animal, and he feared that the free market system could result in new class antagonisms resulting from a widening gap between rich and poor. Smith thus ranks among the greatest economists, not only as founding father and philosopher, but as prophet.

Most important of all, Smith did foresee the fecundity of the free market and a free enterprise system as a source of national wealth. As valuable as the market may be as an allocator of resources and as a promoter of efficiency of growth, however, events of the nineteenth and twentieth centuries have demon-

strated that the existence of markets is no guarantee against
political tyranny. Only yesterday, Nazism and Fascism, the
creatures of systemic breakdown and economic insecurity, led
to the most horrible war in history and to the most bloodthirsty
mass murders ever committed.

Today rising tensions in Africa, the Middle East, Latin
America, and even Western Europe are fresh reminders that the
preservation of political and economic freedom, and peace itself,
depends significantly on the economic security and well-being of
multitudes of people. For us over the long run, the conflicts between rich and poor nations loom as a chronic danger. People
will not accept freedom, whether economic or political, as a
substitute for food, clothing, shelter, and a measure of security.
Indeed it is a cruel paradox that political repression should be
used to protect freedom, because working people will not toler-
ate unemployment and rapid inflation. This is the lesson of
Chile. After 1973 in the wake of the overthrow of Allende, the
Chilean junta sought to cure its economic ills by applying free
enterprise and monetary solutions. In order to do so, however,
the junta stifled the news media and political parties, shackled
labor unions, and employed torture as a political instrument.

Capitalism and freedom are not necessarily inseparable.
Economic institutions never exist in a political vacuum. Every
economy is embedded in a particular polity. The illusion that
economics could be divorced from politics existed for a while
during the nineteenth and twentieth centuries in England and
the United States—a spell of unusually fair weather for laissez-
faire capitalism that has now blown away. This is a time of
much soul searching among economists all over the world, a soul
searching of the philosophical and methodological bases of their
discipline. Many economists today still maintain that economics
is simply a set of analytical techniques applicable to certain
aspects of production, distribution, exchange, and consumption.
They assert that the science of economics aims at increasing the

efficient use of resources and realizing the goals postulated by individuals, businesses, or governments, but that economists as such cannot specify the goals for society. Their science, many economists insist, gives them no means and no special qualifications for doing so, and it would be elitist or authoritarian for them to try.

That economics can or should be value free seems to be an antiseptic way of looking at the task of this discipline, an antiseptic attitude that is no longer shared by most economists including, I would think, Professor Friedman. On the left there is much concern about the role of power in dominating the distribution of income and in directing resources in all societies, even those nominally free of power. It was not exactly a new discovery, even when Marx made it over a century ago, that in many societies there was a class structure. In a famous revolutionary sermon at Blackheath preached during the peasant revolt in England in 1381, John Ball, the lay preacher, declared: "They have wine and spices and fair bread, and we have oatcake and straw and water to drink. They have leisure and fine houses, we have pain and labor, the rain and the wind in the fields, and yet it is of us and our toil that these men hold their estate."

One does not have to be a peasant, a revolutionary, or a Marxist to recognize that class and race and national origin have a good deal to do with the distribution of income at any given time and over centuries of time. Conventional economists through most of the past century have concentrated too narrowly on increasing the efficiency and growth of production, while paying too little attention to the distribution of wealth and income or to the still wider issue of social justice. They have assumed that efficiency was the obvious or implicit objective of their discipline, but that the study of social and economic justice was beyond the reach of economic science. The economists, with rare exceptions, treated equality and inequality, justice and injustice as matters for somebody else, for philosophers, lawyers, or the citizenry in general, but not for themselves as economists. But such recent and sharply contrasting works as those of John Rawls's *Theory of Justice* and Robert Nozick's *Anarchy, State and Utopia,* together with the heightened turmoil and conflict in the real world over equal opportunity and income distribution and demands of the poor nations for a better share, have aroused economists to the need of addressing themselves to the critical questions of justice and equality, and how they relate to such other economic objectives as efficiency, growth, welfare, and freedom—objectives as important now as they ever were. If economists presume to minister to the ills of society, as they do in fact presume, they cannot select only those goals or those values which conveniently fit the traditional concepts and models and data of their discipline.

In my view some economists who consider themselves to be disciples of Adam Smith extend beyond its proper limits the domain of the market. They are trying to revive a system of social values and economic institutions which characterized the United States prior to the New Deal, before the United States and other capitalist nations set out on what Professor Hayek called "The Road to Serfdom." Economic freedom and social justice are two quite different values. Economic freedom is the right of individuals or businesses to act autonomously, free of government constraint or direction. Social justice can most simply be defined as the principle that equals will be treated equally. And just as important is the corollary to that principle: unequals will be treated unequally. Thus, for example, the principle of equity in taxation holds that all people with the same income should pay the same taxes, and people with higher or lower income should pay higher or lower taxes; or under just law people who are found guilty of committing the same crime should receive equal punishment, and people who commit a greater offense should receive greater punishment. Or if there are other factors of inequality, such as age or mental condition, again the treatment shall be unequal. It is important to remember that inequality is as important an element of justice as equality. The crucial question in deciding what contributes to social justice is: What are the essential attributes of equality or inequality? Obviously people are not equal in all respects. Some are taller, heavier, smarter, more ignorant, etc. From the standpoint of law, we in the United States maintain that all citizens are equal and should receive equal treatment no matter what their attribute is, except for minors and so on. But although we say that all people are entitled to equal justice, there has been no presumption in our society that all are entitled to equal economic rewards. We assert that rewards should be proportional to economic contributions, yet many of our institutions—such as the progressive income tax, free public education, welfare payments, food stamps—do imply a national belief that the distribution of income should be made at least somewhat more equal than market forces alone would yield. And we put a floor under the income of many individuals to prevent starvation and utter destitution. Is this as far as we should go, or can we go further in redistributing the fruits of our highly productive economic system without undermining its freedom and its efficiency?

Here is one of the critical and emerging issues of our time, and one that takes many forms not only as economic issues, like tax reform or negative income taxes, to which Professor Friedman has importantly contributed, but also to inheritance laws, welfare payments, and minimum wages, and such social issues as busing and racial integration, school integration, and benign quotas in education or employment. True-blue conservatives have little trouble with such issues. Anything that impairs the efficiency of freedom of the system they say is wrong economically, socially, and morally. They are in the tradition of that nineteenth century champion of laissez-faire Herbert Spencer, who declared, "The command, 'if any would not work, neither should he eat,' is simply a Christian enunciation of the universal law of nature under which life has reached its present height, the law that the creature not energetic enough to maintain itself must die." Spencer was even against free public libraries, on the ground that they gave people something for nothing and encouraged loafing. Latter-day Spencerians see the pursuit of equality as sapping the life of capitalist growth, with socialist Britain as the horrible example of economic decay. On the other side, egalitarians see the ever-expanding market capitalism as the corrupter of human dignity and human rights. Money can buy things that should not be for sale, including justice and political power, and thereby vitiate our formal, national commitments to equal democratic rights for all citizens.

There is a very strong case for the market, in terms of both efficiency and freedom, but I think that one must look at that word "freedom" very carefully, as John Stuart Mill did a century ago. He said:

Trade is a social act. Whoever undertakes to sell and distribute goods to the public does what affects the interest of other people and society in general, and thus, his conduct and principle comes under the jurisdiction of society. Accordingly, it was once held to be the duty of government in all cases which were considered of importance to fix prices and regulate the processes of manufacture. But it is now recognized, though not till after a long struggle, that both the cheapness and good quality of commodities are most effectually provided for by leaving the producers and sellers perfectly free under the sole check of equal freedom for the buyers for supplying themselves elsewhere.

This is the so-called doctrine of free trade, which rests on grounds different from, though equally solid with, the principle of individual liberty asserted in this essay. This is from Mill's essay on *Freedom:*

Restrictions on trade or in the production for purposes of trade
are indeed restraints, and all restraints, qua *restraints are an evil,*
but the restraints in question affect only [here he begins to
wander from the true faith] *that part of conduct which society*
is competent to restrain, and are wrong solely because they do
not really produce the results which·it is desired to produce by
them.

The principle of individual liberty, says Mill, is not involved
in the doctrine of free trade, and neither is it in most of the
questions that arise respecting the limits of the doctrine; for
example, what amount of public control is admissible for the
prevention of fraud by adulteration? How far should sanitary
precautions or arrangements to protect working people employed in dangerous occupations be enforced on employers?
Such questions involve considerations of liberty only insofar as
leaving people to themselves is always better, *ceteris paribus,*
than controlling them. But that they may be legitimately controlled for these ends is, in principle, undeniable. On the other
hand, there are questions relating to interference with trade
which *are* essentially questions of liberty, already touched upon.
The prohibition of the importation of opium into China or the
restriction of the sale of poisons are, says Mill, typical of cases
where the object of the interference is to make it impossible or
difficult to obtain a particular commodity. These interferences
are objectionable as infringements on the liberty not of the
producer or the seller, but of the buyer. Mill now resolves this
Nader-like issue. One of these examples, the sale of poisons,
opens a new question. The proper limits of what may be called
the functions of police, how far liberty may legitimately be in-
vaded for the prevention of crime or of an accident. It is one of
the undisputed functions of government to take precautions
against crime before it has been committed, as well as to detect
and punish it afterward. The preventive function of government,

however, is far more liable to be abused to the prejudice of liberty than the punitive function, for there is hardly a part of the legitimate freedom of action of a human being which would not admit of being represented, and fairly too, as increasing the facilities for some form or other of deliquency. Nevertheless, if a public authority or even a private person sees anyone evidently preparing to commit a crime, he is not bound to look on, inactive, until the crime is committed, but may interfere to prevent it. Says Mill: "If poisons were never bought or used for any purpose except the commission of murders, it would be right to prohibit their manufacture and sale," but of course they are not. Mill sees the conflict between worthy objectives, and that is the essence of the problem of ethics. There is the mind of a man wrestling with real problems, with delicately balanced, conflicting objectives, not the mind of someone who has discovered a gimmick, who has discovered a nice oversimplification of what the moral problem is that confronts society when redress cannot be had after a crime is committed or after a poison has been administered.

Our moral issues are not simple issues. Our moral issues involve conflicts between goods, as Sidney Hook has said, and therefore one must not pretend that there is a simple and universal rule, whatever the rule is, that can resolve such conflicts. But on the other side, of course, we must worry about the state. That was never truer than during the Nixon administration, which prided itself in its belief in the free market. It did more than any other administration, in my history, in my memory, and in my reading, to restore liberals' wariness of the powers of the state. It did that, however, not by preaching but by demonstrating what those evils were. Some businesses, too, have shown, not by their advertisements in newspapers but by their corrupt symbiosis with government, how the life of a free society and a democracy can be endangered by the state.

A lot of time has gone by since Smith, and the revolution

that he foresaw—which was not simply a revolution of free trade as Professor Friedman said, but also an industrial revolution—has come to pass and the face of society has been drastically altered. We have new problems that we cannot forget. One of those problems is that of equality. It is very much the problem of today. The assumption that economic growth would provide people an answer that would keep them content through increased absolute income turns out not to be true. It turns out that in affluent societies the desire for equality increases rather than decreases, and the justification for inequality is greatly weakened. Once the level of living is raised to a certain point, there is no excuse for not sharing with those people who are at the bottom of the ladder, or not worrying about how they can be moved up to a decent level of living. That's true internationally as well as nationally. One can never simply dismiss the issue of equality, least of all in this bicentennial year, the anniversary of the Declaration of Independence, as well as *The Wealth of Nations.* One cannot dismiss equality as a neurosis of liberals, a term sometimes used pejoratively when applied to twentieth-century liberals. Nor can we in a rich society justify our continued neglect or devastation of the social and natural environment in the name of market efficiency or growth. Fortunately, equality and decency are not always in conflict with efficiency or growth. Herbert Spencer was almost certainly wrong, for instance, about the total effect of public libraries. They have surely done more to improve human capital than to breed sloth. The output lost from the waste of human resources is almost certainly greater than the social costs needed to develop them. Efficiency in any case is not an ultimate end but an instrumental value, a tool. Only a mindless and compulsive society could make efficiency the be all and end all of economic and social action. Economics itself appears to be shifting away from such mindlessness, and a good thing it is.

To disentangle the social philosophies or politics of econo-

mists from their economics is extremely difficult. Professor
Friedman and I are two examples of different social philosophies.
Is that fact wrong, or bad, a serious weakness in economics as
such? I think it is a very important question, for the public
grows skeptical of economists when they differ. That is what the
Swedish Academy of Sciences was trying to say in 1974 when it
awarded the Nobel Prize in Economic Science simultaneously to
Gunnar Myrdal, a socialist, a planner, an ignoramus if you believe
some critics of people who believe in planning; and Friedrich
Hayek, a libertarian and a former colleague of Professor Friedman. In fact, both Myrdal and Hayek have stressed the difficulty
or impossibility of purging economic analysis of political, social,
and moral values. Myrdal has contended that problems in the
social sciences—not only the practical ones about what ought to
be done, but also the theoretical problems of ascertaining the
facts and the relations among facts—cannot be rationally posited
except in terms of definite, concretized, and explicit value pre-
mises. And Hayek, in his Nobel Prize lecture, attacked what he
called the "scientistic attitude" of economists, an approach he
said is "decidedly unscientific in the true sense of the word since
it involves a mechanical and uncritical application of habits of
thought to fields different from those in which they have been
formed." The public is, in fact, usually not deceived by some
economists' pretention to scientific purity. It identifies economists, usually correctly, as far right, or conservative, or middle
of the road, or liberal, or leftist; the public knows that this
often, although not necessarily, affects the nature of their
analyses or their recommendations on policy. But the economist
is sometimes self-deceived and only succeeds in lowering his own
standing and that of his profession by seeking to invoke professional authority for his personal values. There is, after all,
nothing wrong with the controversy among economists. Indeed
it is a crucial part of the process by which truth is discovered
and values explicated. That many-sided discourse among the
economists has never been more intense than it is today.

Paul Samuelson notes that the new economics—that is, the
economics of Keynes and Samuelson which still occupies the
middle of the road and the high ground of the economic establishment in the profession—is now under attack on four fronts.
First, from those of conservative interests, whose historic rejec-
tion of any effort to use government economic policy has always
been opposed on blind ideological grounds. That is a position,
incidentally, into which I would certainly not try to thrust
Professor Friedman. I do think that Professor Friedman belongs
in the second category, however, which the term "libertarian"
suits and which reminds us very correctly and very importantly
(if I may say this in public) of the continued importance of the
market, a contribution that fully justifies the Nobel Prize for
my distinguished copanelist. I think that this contribution is
precisely what he has been making today, reminding us what the
market does, what market pricing accomplishes, and what dis-
regarding those lessons, which go back to Adam Smith, leads to.
Thirdly, there is another attack on the establishment, such as
that of Galbraith, of the inadequacies and imperfections of the
market; to that crusade far greater attention to public programs
and public needs is due. And finally, there is the new left, the
children of affluence, who even with Vietnam behind us are
becoming more and more critical of the economic system. So
there is extreme controversy within the economics profession.
I happen to regard that as a sign of health, not of disease.

Out of these many voices of the right, the center, and the
left, does a single economics emerge? In a strange way, I think
that it does. I think that what we have is a dialogue of knowl-
edgeable combatants who know each other's tricks. It can be
said that, at their best and most disinterested, the economists
have sought to understand a very mysterious and vital phenomenon, the economy (Professor Friedman very well described it on
an international level), and have sought to prescribe for its real
and serious ills. When Professor Friedman is not praising the

beauty and perfection of the market, he is trying to prescribe for the ills of the market, although he might not accept my terminology. The economists have sought to shape events rationally in an effort to advance society's welfare as they have variously interpreted it. They have sought to teach society and individual statesmen the truth. These are high and ambitious goals which, however short of them economists may have fallen, make far more sense than trusting to the blind forces of history. Adam Smith's great work was, as Professor Friedman said, a tract for reform, not a plea for submission to fate, to blind fate. Invisible hands, we have learned in this century, can lead us to tyranny as well as to freedom and social welfare. Our goals must be the conscious goals of intelligent human beings, and they must be social goals, not merely the goals of self-interest.

Part Two
Modern Institutions and Individual Freedom:
Thomas Jefferson Plus Two Hundred Years

3. SUITING THE JOB
TO THE PERSON:
THE VOLVO EXPERIENCE

Pehr G. Gyllenhammar

Pehr G. Gyllenhammar is President of AB Volvo, in Gothen-burg, Sweden, where he was born in 1935. Before becoming head of the Volvo group of companies in 1971, he had been President of Skandia, Sweden's largest insurance company. Trained as a lawyer, he has gained international repute for his humanistic concerns for the quality of the work environment, demonstrated most vividly in Volvo's innovative car assembly plant in Kalmar, Sweden, where new technology and work procedures have replaced the traditional assembly line.

THE AMOS TUCK SCHOOL has devoted its efforts for seventy-five years to upgrade and prepare well educated people to do a good job in management. Whoever is involved in management realizes that we spend almost endless efforts to make the lives of our top executives interesting—inventing stock options and incentive schemes, for example, to retain them in our businesses. Yet hardly any time is spent improving job interest for the majority of our work force. Research people in universities find it difficult even to obtain data on this matter and in no small part because of top management's lack of cooperation. The little research that has been done has been of doubtful quality. It is still basically true that, as Adam Smith said, "a worker gives up his ease, his liberty and his happiness when he goes into industry."

Mr. Pehr Gustav Gyllenhammar.

Freedom is, of course, relative, and we are dealing in semantics or symbols when we talk about the free world. But however we look at it, we may agree that freedom is partly a freedom to move—a certain mobility. There are places in the world where a major part of the population cannot physically move. They are so impoverished that they would not move if they could. Yet freedom to move, and mobility, are extremely important. Why is it that most workers in the industrialized

world have this freedom of mobility outside their work but
not inside? They are tied down by procedures, and they are
tied down physically. Typically, a blue-collar worker has
performance standards to meet more or less every minute of
the day; whereas a white-collar worker, who has very few performance standards, can spend half of the day away from his
desk and nobody really cares. Real freedom, including the freedom to move, does not exist for blue-collar workers, who therefore are apt to develop negative attitudes toward developing
themselves, or devoting much of their effort toward developing
the corporation.

There are restrictions on all of us—because of technology,
of size or scale. Many people are today frustrated by urban
development. They are frustrated by the size of their work
places. We have a lot of evidence that workers accept their
situation much better in a small work place than in a big one.
The bigger places very often afford a better physical environment, but probably the social environment in the small work
place is so important that it easily compensates for the poor
physical environment.

In my home country we provide today a basic education
with an average duration of some ten to twelve years. Less than
two decades ago, people had a basic education of fewer than
seven years. Yet we give them more or less the same jobs now as
then. What has changed? As far as business organizations are
concerned, nothing has changed. If you go to the management
literature, or most of it, you will find it talking in terms of the
organizational structures we have been discussing since the
1930's. When we talk about decentralization, people still refer to
Sloan's book *My Years with General Motors.* Very little is really
new. We allocate massive funds and resources for a basic education, and we don't utilize it except on the higher levels in industry. I believe that even though many people complain about the
new educational systems and say that they don't provide the

competence and the skills that we should expect from so much
more education, they give people changed values. Normally
people go on strike for money. You don't go on strike because
you are just plain bored with your job; in that case you leave
the organization—if, of course, you have other options.

We had this phenomenon in our corporation toward the
end of the 1960's. It peaked in 1970, when the turnover of
workers was extremely high. At that time I visited a few American colleagues and asked them about their turnover. They said
it was no problem. I was amazed, because I had visited some of
the plants there and received different information. When you
turn out products every day which are shipped every day, with
the same procedures, when people do repetitive things day in
and day out, year by year, you wonder how long workers can
continue doing these things. These top managers had no problem
because in the big metropolitan areas where there was a good
supply of labor, people were leaving but replacements were
being quickly trained. The problems were being experienced by
plant managers and by the workers themselves. So a closer in-
vestigation showed in fact that their turnover figures were the
same as ours: 50 percent every year. That to me is horrifying. It
made us wonder if this system would collapse one day. It should
collapse. There was no correlation between what we were offering people outside of work, what we seemed to offer them by
giving them a good education, and what they were actually left
with after the age of 19. Their career is a straight line from 19 to
65, doing exactly the same thing every day, and that is not
acceptable if you accept the fact that people have an enormous
potential for development. This, I think, gets us down to at least
equality of opportunity. That is very hard to provide, but we
have made a modest start.

It is easy to be cynical about change in the nature of work.
I'm not. I see it in practice, and I started out by saying that we
have, in a broad perspective, made some changes. It is almost

embarrassing to note how much attention has been given to such modest changes, but it would be more embarrassing not to have tried at all. I think the most important thing we have done is not to experiment, as many people call it, but to have committed ourselves to new solutions. There is no way back, even if we wanted to change our minds. We now have, for example, a plant designed for a specific purpose. If the system does not work, it is a failure in economic and social terms. We now have four new plants organized in a nontraditional way, besides changes in job design which have taken place in most of our old plants. The object of the new workshops is not to be less productive, but to be more productive, by upgrading jobs and being willing and motivated to do still more.

The bottleneck seemed to us to be the technology itself. You can make a corporation spend almost any amount of money on marketing and sales promotion these days without any evidence whatsoever that it will buy something. If you ask corporations to stop spending or to cut their spending on advertising, even the top executives feel uneasy. The best if not only way to measure advertising is to stop doing it, but you don't dare, because if the effects are bad, you will be blamed. When a technology works, it is hard to convince executives to spend one penny on change. The breakthrough, the innovation, that the assembly line brought about was mass production of complex mechanical products. It has worked well. For better or worse, I have been motivated to try to change it, and am on the record as believing that you cannot reorganize you work force *unless* you change it. We broke up the line, to put it simply, by not using conveyors going through a warehouse, which is what an assembly plant is, but by designing individual carriers for the product. These carriers can move very freely in a layout that is not determined by their technology. Because you have many individual carriers, you can move them and stop them independently of one another. The first humiliation that meets man or woman in an assembly plant is that one has to run after the product. Imagine every working day of you life running after a product. Yet few have questioned the necessity for it. *We* have said that if you, a worker, are profit-oriented, perhaps you will do a better job if the product stays put and you can work on it and concentrate on it rather than running after it. Secondly, we have identified and done something about the social component. People need to have social contact. Even if it is very quiet in the conventional plant, people are physically isolated from one another. They are so busy working at "short tempos" (perhaps 30 or 60 seconds) that they cannot communicate and must have their social life outside the working environment instead of communicating on their jobs. They cannot even communicate on matters relating to their job, for they are encouraged not to talk. So we said, bring them together; in a collective effort they could do much more. Let them work as a group assembling a chassis, for example, and decide for themselves how to organize the work.

We have four plants where we have tried variations of this technology. Initially we have concentrated on only one thing, not to motivate people but to make the technical systems work. Why? Because if we failed with the technical systems, many of our critics would say they were a complete failure. If we succeed with them, we will succeed economically. People don't care too much about other people, sad to say. If we succeed with people, it will not interest them much. But if we succeed technically and economically first, I have the strong belief that out of this will come a sense of liberation that will motivate people to do a better job for us. The best we can hope for in plants where tech-nology does not limit the freedom of man or woman is that we will have a new dynamism in organizational development which will come from the work force. But that will be enough to start, for then we will have an organization that is really new and has the ability of renewing itself. People ask me, if you have achieved initially good results, isn't it natural that they are the result of the newness of the beautiful environment? That is a very odd remark. I reply, so what? If this is what people want, introduce novelties of the kind that people will want to live with. That is one of the main responsibilities of management. If we set graduates of Amos Tuck to doing the same things all their lives, they will be terribly disappointed. Part of the problem of motivation is how to introduce change in life, change controlled by man. There are two ways to do it: to have enlightened management that is devoted to the effort, and, still better, to have the people who can take the opportunities you give them to provide a technology that gives the freedom of, at least, mobility that makes them think, and that does use their potential to do much more important things for their organizations in the future.

This so-called Swedish model, where employees are beginning to participate in managerial decisions, is more than just an invention due to pressures from labor unions. Sensibly used, I think it is one of the few tools to really move an organization in the future. We have in our company a few things that we have introduced deliberately and voluntarily without pressure of legislation or without pressure from unions. We invited four representatives of the workers and the employees to participate on our Board of Directors before this became law. Perhaps our critics could say that was one of the reasons why the legislators decided to introduce it. Anyway, it has worked very well for us. The presence of members of the work force does keep one extremely honest. And it keeps them honest too, because all the rhetoric of the bargaining procedure is gone when they sit in the board room. They, of course, are at a disadvantage because their basic education is not the same. They don't know the jargon of the economists and the technicians. But they learn, and they know a lot of other things that the other directors don't know, and there is a mutual respect. We have had very few conflicts and we have had to make decisions on difficult issues.

We have a Group Works Council, which I chair. We have works councils all through the organization. This is regulated by collective agreement, although they are not unique for any Swedish corporation. But the Group Works Council is unique in that I meet directly with our people frequently. In two cases I have asked them to advise us at a very early stage. The first was about our investment in the United States, on which they were asked to comment and consider this whole issue several months before the matter was brought to our Board of Directors. The other was about an acquisition of a Dutch affiliate of ours, a producer of small cars even smaller than our traditional cars. In both instances, the issue involved for the Swedish work force was one of employment. If we put up an assembly plant in the United States, which is a country of free trade with very low tariffs, it would be a strategic investment, not a necessarily financially good or economically good investment in the short term. Certainly it would mean that jobs that could have been created in Sweden were being created in the United States instead. It was a straight transfer of jobs from their point of view. They discussed this for about two to three months. I did not give them the right of veto, and they have not got it now, but in essence what I did was the same thing, for had they come our strongly against it, I think the issue would have been dead. As it happened they backed the project from beginning to end.

In the second instance—namely, the fairly substantial investment, by our standards, in Holland—the Group Works Council came out in exactly the same way. They visited independently, at our expense, and they were asked to visit if they wished, the Dutch organization. They had plenty of time to discuss the issue with the Dutch. They recommended that we go ahead. They thought that our program would be broadened and strengthened, so they said they were all for it, and the Board's decision was made easier.

I mention this because some people talk about our country

as an example where management control, in the traditional sense, may be lost and where participation by workers will lead to a reduced efficiency for corporations. I think a loss in efficiency for corporations may well be seen in a number of cases but that, in my opinion, it will be due to poor management rather than that the system has been changed so as to obstruct the development of corporations. There is a broad misunderstanding when it comes to dealing with union people, and particularly your own employees—namely, that you have to become steadily more permissive. That is a complete misunderstanding. I think you have to be more disciplined and stronger. Only the weak people in our management have difficulties in dealing with employee representatives, primarily because they do not have their employees' respect. The strong leaders who have the strength to give and who have the strength to talk about their mistakes do have their respect. Only then can you move. That is what an important part of our management effort is about.

4. ADAM SMITH AS MANAGEMENT THEORIST

Eli Ginzberg

Eli Ginzberg is Professor of Economics in the Graduate School of Business, Columbia University, and Director of the Conservation of Human Resources. He has been a member of the Columbia University faculty for forty years. In addition to heading the oldest disciplinary team in the field of human resources and manpower, dating back to 1939, which has resulted in the publication of more than eighty books, he has been an active consultant to the federal government since 1941, having served the last seven presidents. He is currently Chairman of the National Commission for Manpower Policy.

ADAM SMITH had no illusions that although people make gains as a result of working, they also make sacrifices when they accept employment. "In his ordinary state of health, strength and dexterity he must always lay down the same portion of his ease, his liberty, and his happiness" (*Wealth of Nations,* Modern Library, page 33). These are not unimportant or incidental sacrifices. When a worker accepts a job, he gives up control over his time, his energies, himself.

Smith was not sentimental. Unlike present-day consultants, who seek to persuade prospective customers that they can contribute to the morale and productivity of the work force by rearrangements that will add to the prestige of work held in low esteem and extract the unpleasantness out of dirty and routine jobs, Smith saw little point in denying the obvious. He said: "In

Dr. Eli Ginzberg.

the inferior employments, the sweets of labor consist almost altogether in the recompense of labor" (122). On the basis of this insight, Smith argued in favor of reducing the time of apprenticeship, believing that it would help to form young people to industry if they were paid sooner rather than later. Those who, like Milton Friedman and Martin Feldstein, are convinced that a high level of youth unemployment can be cured by reducing the wages of young people, might well ponder this observation of Adam Smith.

Too little attention has been paid by economists, particularly those concerned with economic development, to another of Smith's insights. He saw the prosperity of Great Britain in terms "of the security of enjoying the fruits of labor." This was his explication of this basic theorem:

The natural effort of every individual to better his own condition, when suffered to exert itself with freedom and security, is so powerful a principle, that it is alone, and without any assistance, not only capable of carrying on the society to wealth and prosperity, but of surmounting a hundred impertinent obstructions with which the folly of human laws too often incumbers its operations; though the effect of these obstructions is always more or less either to encroach upon its freedom, or to diminish its security. In Great Britain industry is perfectly secure; and though it is far from being perfectly free, it is as free or freer than in any other part of Europe. (508)

I would like to add personal testimony to this formulation. In my view the excessive inflation in Germany of 1922–23, which robbed hard-working men and women of their life-time savings, prepared the ground for Hitler. In 1966, while I was on a study mission in Ethiopia, I discovered that as soon as migrant workers on coffee plantations were paid, they spent their wages on orgies; they had learned that if they had money with them when they returned home, they would be charged with a trumped-up crime and would have to give their savings to the authorities. My third example derives from a recent visit to Italy. If the 20 percent annual inflation rate which has been in effect for the last three years continues much longer—and I do not see how it can be stopped—I do not believe that the Communists can be excluded from the government.

There are two more passages from *The Wealth of Nations* that bear on Smith's view of the worker. The first deals with wages; the second concerns application or, to use the word in vogue today, motivation.

The notation along the margin of Smith's opus puts the wage issue succinctly: "High wages encourage industry." The key sentences of this crucial paragraph follow:

The wages of labour are the encouragement of industry, which, like every other human quality, improves in proportion to the encouragement it receives. A plentiful subsistence increases the bodily strength of the labourer, and the comfortable hope of bettering his condition, and of ending his days perhaps in ease and plenty animates him to exert that strength to the utmost. Where wages are high, accordingly, we shall always find the workmen more active, diligent, and expeditious, than where they are low; in England, for example, than in Scotland; in the neighbourhood of great towns, than in remote country places. (81)

In the second part of this long paragraph, Smith speaks to the issue of whether workers are industrious or lazy. In consonance with his general approach—minimizing in-born traits and seeing the environment as determining patters of behavior —Smith adumbrates the principle that if men want to improve their condition, they are more likely to overwork than opt for leisure:

Some workmen, indeed, when they can earn in four days what will maintain them through the week, will be idle the other three. This, however, is by no means the case with the greater part. Workmen, on the contrary, when they are liberally paid by the piece, are very apt to over-work themselves, and to ruin their health and constitution in a few years. A carpenter in London, and in some other places, is not supposed to last in his utmost vigour above eight years. Something of the same kind happens in many other trades, in which the workmen are paid by the piece; as they generally are in manufactures, and even in country labour, wherever wages are higher than ordinary. Almost every class of artificers is subject to some peculiar infirmity

occasioned by excessive application to their peculiar species of
work ... Excessive application during four days of the week, is
frequently the real cause of the idleness of the other three, so
much and so loudly complained of. (81, 82)

Since I did not have the opportunity to hear Milton Friedman yesterday afternoon, I must rely on what I know of the
Chicago School. I assume he suggested that employers pursue
their search for profits in as effective a manner as possible. But
for Smith such a preoccupation is not enough. Near the end of
the above cited paragraph, he added the following advice: "If
masters would always listen to the dictates of reason and humanity, they would have frequently occasion rather to moderate,
than to animate the application of many of their workmen" (82).

The foregoing quotations are no more than hors d'oeuvres
for the rich feast that Smith sets out in *The Wealth of Nations*
about the overweening importance of the role of the individual
in the shaping and performance of the economy and society. He
appreciated what so many of his successors overlooked—namely,
that the individual is never an isolated atom but is always an
integral part of a social environment which, at one and the same
time, offers him opportunities and constrains him with respect
to his options and accomplishments. Let us look at certain other
passages where Smith assesses how different work environments
impact those exposed to them. We will deal sequentially with
four: the environment of the industrial worker, the farmer, the
professor, and the manager.

By the way of introduction to the industrial-work environment, we must recall that Smith saw the division of labor as the
principal mechanism responsible for increasing productivity and
the accumulation of wealth. Division of labor, Smith contended,
is not an incidental process but is of paramount importance in
the material progress of mankind. Therefore, it is remarkable
that Smith was uneasy about the consequences of the division
of labor for both the individual and the nation. Once again there

is an overview of Smith's position in the margin of his text: "Division of labour destroys intellectual, social, and martial virtues unless government takes pains to prevent it" (734). I must call attention to the fact that the great advocate of laissez-faire did not hesitate in giving government a major role to play in preventing the destruction of both men and society!

The whole of his argument about the dysfunctional nature of the division of labor is important:

In the progress of the division of labour, the employment of the far greater part of those who live by labour, that is, of the great body of the people, comes to be confined to a few very simple operations, frequently to one or two. But the understandings of the greater part of men are necessarily formed by their ordinary employments. The man whose whole life is spent in performing a few simple operations, of which the effects too are, perhaps, always the same, or very nearly the same, has no occasion to exert his understanding, or to exercise his invention in finding out expedients for removing difficulties which never occur. He naturally loses, therefore, the habit of such exertion, and generally becomes as stupid and ignorant as it is possible for a human creature to become. The torpor of his mind renders him, not only incapable of relishing or bearing a part in any rational conversation, but of conceiving any generous, noble, or tender sentiment, and consequently of forming any just judgment concerning many even of the ordinary duties of private life. Of the great and extensive interests of his country he is altogether incapable of judging; and unless very particular pains have been taken to render him otherwise, he is equally incapable of defending his country in war. The uniformity of his stationary life naturally corrupts the courage of his mind, and makes him regard with abhorrence the irregular, uncertain, and adventurous life of a soldier. It corrupts even the activity of his body, and renders him incapable of exerting his strength with vigour and perseverance, in any other employment than that to which he has been bred.

His dexterity at his own particular trade seems, in this manner, to be acquired at the expence of his intellectual, social, and martial virtues. But in every improved and civilized society this is the state into which the labouring poor, that is, the great body of the people, must necessarily fall, unless government takes some pains to prevent it. (734-735)

According to Smith the consequences of further acceleration of the division of labor would lead to more material accumulation, but at the same time it would speed the degradation of the laboring poor—that is, the great body of the people. Contemporary social science has traced the doctrine of alienation and dehumanization back to Karl Marx. Apparently present-day ideologists could not conceive that the father of modern capitalism, as they see Smith, could possibly have been alert to dangers incident to the extreme division of labor and at the same time have sounded the alarm for governmental action to counter its deleterious effects.

What about the environment in which the farmer works? The following encapsulates Smith's views:

Not only the art of the farmer, the general direction of the operations of husbandry, but many inferior branches of country labour, require much more skill and experience than the greater part of mechanic trades. The man who works upon brass and iron, works with instruments and upon materials of which the temper is always the same, or very nearly the same. But the man who ploughs the ground with a team of horses or oxen, works with instruments of which the health, strength, and temper, are very different upon different occasions. The condition of the materials which he works upon too is as variable as that of the instruments which he works with, and both require to be managed with much judgment and discretion. The common ploughman, though generally regarded as the pattern of stupidity and ignorance, is seldom defective in this judgment and discretion.

He is less accustomed, indeed, to social intercourse than the
mechanic who lives in a town. His voice and language are more
uncouth and more difficult to be understood by those who are
not used to them. His understanding, however, being accustomed
to consider a greater variety of objects, is generally much superior
to that of the other, whose whole attention from morning till
night is commonly occupied in performing one or two very sim-
ple operations. How much the lower ranks of people in the coun-
try are really superior to those of the town, is well known to
every man whom either business or curiosity has led to converse
much with both. (127)

Those who compare the industrial laborer to the farmer
almost without exception see the laborer as the more sophisticated, the more competent. But not Smith. He looks beyond
surface differences and finds that in terms of skill and competence the farmer is clearly the stronger. And the same type of
incisiveness characterizes Smith's critique of professors, an occu-
pation with which he was intimately acquainted.

Smith's analysis of academics begins by differentiating those
whose income depends in whole or part on fees from students
(whom they must attract and hold) from those who receive a
salary. In the latter instance, Smith sees little involvement and
less output by faculty members. To quote him directly:

His interest is, in this case, set as directly in opposition to his
duty as it is possible to set it. It is the interest of every man to
live as much at his ease as he can; and if his emoluments are to
be precisely the same, whether he does, or does not perform
some very laborious duty, it is certainly his interest, at least as
interest is vulgarly understood, either to neglect it altogether,
or, if he is subject to some authority which will not suffer him
to do this, to perform it in as careless and slovenly a manner as
that authority will permit. If he is naturally active and a lover of
labour, it is his interest to employ that activity in any way, from

which he can derive some advantage, rather than in the perfor-
mance of his duty, from which he can derive none.

If the authority to which he is subject resides in the body
corporate, the college, or university, of which he himself is a
member, and in which the greater part of the other members
are, like himself, persons who either are, or ought to be teachers;
they are likely to make a common cause, to be all very indulgent
to one another, and every man to consent that his neighbour
may neglect his duty, provided he himself is allowed to neglect
his own. In the university of Oxford, the greater part of the
public professors have, for these many years, given up altogether
even the pretence of teaching. (718)

I recall that, in my graduate student days when Adolf Berle
and Gardner Means were finishing *The Modern Corporation and
Private Property,* they considered their book to be the same
genre as *The Wealth of Nations.* Not only were they immodest
(although theirs was an important contribution), but their central
thesis had been adumbrated by Smith a century and a half earlier.
In his analysis of the East India Company, Smith called attention to the fact that "All members of the administration, besides,
trade more or less upon their own account. Nothing can be more
completely foolish than to expect that clerks of a government
counting house at ten thousand miles distance ... should ...
abandon ... all hopes of making a fortune ... and content themselves with the moderate salaries which their masters allow them
(603). Here is the prototype of Berle's and Means's distinction
between owners and management, though Smith referred to
them as masters and clerks!

Another observation of Smith's about a characterological
fault in managers warrants attention: "The pride of man makes
him love to domineer, and nothing mortifies him so much as to
be obliged to condescend to persuade his inferiors" (365).

My third and final theme concerns the ties between *The
Wealth of Nations* and the American Revolution. Specifically,

how did Smith explain the thrust to independence by the
colonies and what advice did he offer his countrymen with regard to how best to respond to the rebellion?

Smith has a distinctive explanation for the source of the
rebellion. His explanation is rooted not in economics, nor in
politics, but in the vanity of leaders.

*Should the parliament of Great Britain, at the same time, be
ever fully established in the right of taxing the colonies, even
independent of the consent of their own assemblies, the importance of those assemblies would from that moment be at an
end, and with it, that of all leading men of British America. Men
desire to have some share in the management of public affairs
chiefly on account of the importance which it gives them. Upon
the power which the greater part of the leading men, the natural
aristocracy of every country, have of preserving or defending
their respective importance, depends the stability and duration
of every system of free government. In the attacks which those
leading men are continually making upon the importance of one
another, and in the defence of their own, consists the whole
play of domestic faction and ambition. The leading men of
America, like those of all other countries, desire to preserve
their own importance. They feel, or imagine, that if their
assemblies, which they are fond of calling parliaments, and of
considering as equal in authority to the parliament of Great
Britain, should be so far degraded as to become the humble
ministers and executive officers of that parliament, the greater
part of their own importance would be at an end. They have
rejected, therefore, the proposal of being taxed by parliamen-
tary requisition, and like other ambitious and high-spirited men,
have rather chosen to draw the sword in defence of their own
importance. (586-587)*

The ties between the two, between *The Wealth of Nations*
and the American Revolution, were much closer than most

people have appreciated. This is evidenced by the fact that Smith ended his opus by offering his countrymen advice about how to respond to the challenge from across the Atlantic. This is how Smith perceived the realistic alternatives facing Parliament and King George III:

The rulers of Great Britain have, for more than a century past, amused the people with the imagination that they possessed a great empire on the west side of the Atlantic. This empire, however, has hitherto existed in imagination only. It has hitherto been, not an empire, but the project of an empire; not a gold mine, but the project of a gold mine; a project which has cost, which continues to cost, and which, if pursued in the same way as it has been hitherto, is likely to cost, immense expence, without being likely to bring any profit; for the effects of the monopoly of the colony trade, it has been shewn, are, to the great body of the people, mere loss instead of profit. It is surely now time that our rulers should either realize this golden dream, in which they have been indulging themselves, perhaps, as well as the people; or, that they should awake from it themselves, and endeavour to awaken the people. If the project cannot be completed, it ought to be given up. If any of the provinces of the British empire cannot be made to contribute towards the support of the whole empire, it is surely time that Great Britain should free herself from the expence of defending those provinces in time of war, and of supporting any part of their civil or military establishments in time of peace, and endeavour to accommodate her future views and designs to the real mediocrity of her circumstances. (899–900)

We are now at the end. I hope that I have fulfilled my promise that I would not traverse the ground which you covered yesterday. And I hope that I will have succeeded in whetting your interest in reading *The Wealth of Nations,* at least in sampling it. And, most importantly, I hope that you will remember that the advocate of laissez-faire that Adam Smith surely was did not see the economy as an end in itself or man as an accumulating automaton who worked to save so as to consume at some future date. Smith was first and foremost a political economist full of advice about how the malfunctioning British economy could be improved; he held that the test of improvement is the capacity of the economy to add to the wealth of the nation reflected in the expanded well-being of its people.

Part Three
Technology for Man:
Benjamin Franklin Plus Two Hundred Years

5. A FEW SCRIBBLES THAT CHANGED THE WORLD

Edward E. David, Jr.

Edward E. David, Jr., is Executive Vice President of Gould, Inc., Chicago, Illinois, responsible for research and development. Before he joined Gould in 1973, he served as science adviser to the President of the United States, and as Director of the Office of Science and Technology, from 1970 through 1972. Prior to that, he was Executive Director for Research at Bell Telephone Laboratories; and he also served as a Professor of Electrical Engineering at Stevens Institute of Technology.

UNCOVERING HISTORY is almost as uncertain as predicting the future. That point is brought out clearly in Arthur Schlesinger's recent review of Woodward and Bernstein's *The Final Days.* Schlesinger points out that "for a historian, there is no democracy of facts which are born free and equal" and, "every good journalist-historian must have in him at least some ingredients of the psychologist, philosopher, and social analyst." This means that significant history requires a sophisticated interpretation of evidence, a task that requires inspiration, just as prediction does. We cannot know all of the past, and we cannot know much of the future.

Yet it is clear that by asking how we got where we are, we may discover significant fundamentals, durable and unchanging, which are likely to influence the future. The one fundamental that has always intrigued me was brought out recently in a

Dr. Edward E. David, Jr.

charming way by an eminent mathematician in his memoirs. The
man is Stanislas Ulam, a Polish-American protégé of John von
Neumann. He played an important role in the creation of the
H-bomb. The statistical techniques he created for modeling the
nuclear fusion processes are now widely used in almost all
branches of science and technology. Ulam, in his book, dwells
upon the startling fact that mathematics can accurately model

events in the real world. This surprising correspondence never fails to amaze and intrigue the students who recognize it. It is one of the most elegant and useful aspects of modern science and technology. It is through this correspondence between symbols, thought, and actuality that science and technology impact our world. Ulam puts it nicely in his book. He says that he has never ceased to be amazed at "how a few scribbles on a blackboard could change the course of human affairs." Indeed, scribbles, augmented by experiment, have been the most revolutionary force in history—have, in fact, largely determined the shape of the world today. Thus scientists and engineers scribble and experiment and the genetic code is broken, the copying industry is created, people by the millions travel and experience foreign cultures, and smallpox is wiped out. This is the awesome power of science and technology—this is the fundamental that is durable and lasting.

This view of human capability to mold the future through the combination of symbol manipulation and experiment is not new in American society. Thomas Jefferson's "knowledge is power" was significantly quoted by President Ford when he signed the bill restoring the Science Adviser to the White House staff. This renewed recognition of science and technology's place in the nation is satisfying to many of us in the technical community. But there is a sobering note.

Recognition of the power of scribbles and experiments says nothing about human and social values, and therefore nothing about whether this power will produce admirable or baleful effects. Any perspective on science and technology, past and future, without a deep consideration of this issue is woefully incomplete.

There are some hopeful signs. In contrast with the common view only a few years ago, we now acknowledge that science and technology are not all powerful. The "technological fix"—the notion that technology alone is the key to society's ills—is becoming passé. We now know that technology is only one ingredient in social situations. For example, technology has provided new possibilities for both increased energy supply and energy conservation, but economic incentives, capital funding, legal regulations, and public consent are required to bring new possibilities into use. Without them technology will often be futile, unused, or, worse, misused. Indeed, economic, legal, social, moral, and political factors world wide are becoming inextricably entwined with science and technology.

Recognition that technology does not always take us where we want to go has led to antitechnological attitudes in some segments of society. The antitechnology movement arises mainly in the developed world, and has become increasingly overt and intellectually respectable in the past ten years. Antitechnology is latent in Lord Snow's "two cultures." The humanities culture has become antitechnological because it is concerned about the effects of pollution from manufacturing enterprises; because of weapons technology and the arms race, with its major call on public resources; and because of the Vietnam War and the SST debate. The intellectual base of the antitechnology movement goes to the nature of people themselves, and the notion that the noblest and most fundamental aspect of human nature is not its rational but its emotional side. These ideas have a devoted following in the world today.

Arrayed against this view is much of public opinion in the West. Opinion surveys indicate that people generally believe that both science and technology have done more to improve humankind's lot than to degrade it. Furthermore, scientists and engineers are held in greater respect than people in most other callings.

It appears to be true that science and technology have had a profound impact on human nature itself. The theme that technology has changed human nature is a popular one among sociologists, amateur and professional. Marshall McLuhan pointed out some years ago the important role of television and modern graphics in this respect. Alvin Toffler takes up a similar idea in his *Future Shock,* when he points out that rapid technological change can and sometimes does induce a neurotic "equal and opposite reaction" against itself. People do not seem to want rapid changes in their lives. Close examination of this thesis by social scientists indicates, however, that reaction to change probably has more to do with the source than with change itself. When people feel they are participating in the implementation of changes in their lives, they can and do adapt very well to profound changes. They rebel when they feel change is being forced on them. So, overall, technology seems to have changed mankind for the better, from a collection of brutes to a much more diverse cohort. I am reminded of that famous scene from the movie *2001* where prehistoric man discovers how to use tools, and subsequently is confronted by the awesome spector of technology in the form of a massive stela.

Nevertheless, there have been many instances in which the side effects of technology have caused human difficulties. This situation is reflected in laws and regulations, such as those aimed at assuring occupational safety, environmental conservation, pure foods and drugs, elections uninfluenced by premature projections, and control of aircraft noise. The process of anticipating side effects before technology is deployed has come to be known as "technology assessment." The Congress has an office to undertake it.

One can hardly object to attempts to head off detrimental effects; yet the very attempt raises a fundamental issue: will technology assessment become technology arrest? Under present auspices, this seems unlikely, for the head of that Congressional office and the originator of the idea itself, former Congressman Emilio Daddario, is currently President of the American Association for the Advancement of Science.

There is on the other hand a certain wariness of technology, a lack of a venturesome spirit in the public temper at the moment. I believe this is a transient situation, for the traditional attitude of the public has been one of adventure and progress, rather than preservation of the status quo. That attitude is as fundamental to the American character as our great inventors, Jefferson, Franklin, Bell, Edison, the Wright brothers, Kettering, and Whitney, are to American history. That character will endure.

Hopeful signs also appear associated with another fundamental—the matter of scale. Schumacher's theme, "small is beautiful," has been true in some areas of technology—for example, computer hardware—and there are some interesting parallels. The subject is a sign of the times. Schumacher and others are pointing out that small, self-contained technology has much to recommend it in some areas of the world. Some people go further and maintain that we should be turning away from large interconnected, interdependent enterprises with high overhead costs, whether in government, industry, or other areas. They advocate more independence, self-sufficiency, and simplicity. This view has a certain appeal for Americans because we have a traditional distrust of concentrations of power. But when it comes to specifics, the subject becomes complex.

Take, for example, the solar heating and cooling of buildings. The technology is certainly available, though it has not been adequately tested on a large scale. Solar collectors, hot water systems for heating and for storage during night-time and cloudy days, and absorption air conditioners all can be bought, though the systems engineering required for widespread installation is still in a primitive state. Furthermore, experience has shown that prudence requires a back-up system of a conventional type with its obvious dependence upon centralized fuel supply of some sort. All of this means that solar heating and cooling of buildings is expensive and does not give the absolute independence that advocates would like. Of course, it can be the only recourse in geographically isolated places. More to the point, a certain amount of *apparent* independence is important to today's psyche.

The proclaimed government slogan "energy independence" is in the same category. Actually, we are unlikely to be truly independent of the rest of the world at any time in the foreseeable future—and there are well established economic, political, and natural resource reasons why that would be undesirable. The desire for energy independence in a literal sense has rightly been called a policy of "drain America first." However, that viewpoint does not recognize the importance of maintaining for our own satisfaction at least an illusion or a fall-back level of self-sufficiency and self-reliance. Those qualities are imprinted deeply on the national conscience and won't be erased. Thus we should expect to see actions that will decrease our dependence upon outside energy supply in easily perceived ways—for example, stockpiling of over one half a billion barrels of oil probably in artificial underground caverns in certain salt dome formations. Such actions give talking points for political forces without any basic change in the supply situation. More importantly, it gives the casual observer a feeling of greater security.

This point about the importance of *perceived* independence as opposed to *real* independence is going to be even more important in the future. Significantly, science and technology are now pointing toward that goal. For example, that monument to the art of the integrated circuit, the microprocessor, makes it eminently feasible to relieve the monotonous uniformity of mass-produced products. It is now feasible to have the best of both economics-of-scale and custom tailoring. The long-promised, mass-produced, custom-tailored product is clearly the wave of the merchandising future.

Similarly, integrated circuits and computer technology promise to upgrade the quality and reliability of products. There will be less and less need for the repairman and less aggravation when technology breaks down. The emphasis is passing from purely increased performance—higher, faster, and further—to increased serviceability, reliability, and affordability. Technology and science will therefore be providing a substantial buffer between our perceptions of our own individual independence and the necessary large-scale enterprises behind our economy and society.

This idea leads to still another area of concern: innovation and its relation to diversity in our society. Innovation in the economy is the process of coupling science and technology to the needs of people and so to commercial markets. It involves a chain that goes far beyond science and technology alone and must include manufacturing, marketing, financing, distribution, servicing, support, and disposal. Innovation is difficult, since it means matching actual technologic possibilities with important human needs through an extremely complex delivery chain. Furthermore, human needs are volatile and can change more rapidly than technology can. We are only beginning to learn how to make the innovation chain responsive to the larger goals of society while at the same time preserving the spontaneity which is essential to its success.

Significantly, we are seeing government intervention in that chain to a very high degree. This intervention is on two levels— one, stimulation of the chain, as ERDA is attempting toward energy innovation—and, two, regulation of innovation through rules, standards, and testing requirements—for example, in the regulation of foods and drugs. In many ways these interventions seem antagonists to each other and provide the base for much of the controversy and adversary proceedings that are so well publicized. In any case, we can be certain that just as the federal government has been a major factor in bringing science and technology into a kind of unity, so the government is going to have its hand in transforming the innovation chain.

Again, we cannot predict the details of this federal influence. But we can say that it has the potential of affecting the very fabric of personal and institutional freedom and self-determination. Just as Jefferson could scarcely have envisioned today's complex system for using knowledge, so it would have been difficult for him to see this coupling between personal freedom of action and innovation. In its major form, this coupling is deceptively simple. Since the innovation chain will determine the life styles of the future, government regulation of that chain can determine the *allowable* future life styles. The danger, of course, is less that of a despotic government than of a benign uniformity imposed through regulations which, though well intended, are inappropriate for the most challenging and intellectually advanced innovations. Rules, standards, and regulations can at best be suitable for a majority of cases. They are likely to impede just those extraordinary initiatives which suddenly appear from knowledge newly acquired. This larger effect of overall regulation has been called the "tyranny of aggregation." It has generated a call for an innovation impact statement before regulations can be promulgated.

Regulation is one dimension of government intervention. The other is federally funded Research and Development aimed at producing for the general commercial marketplace. One measure of that increasing mode of activity is the $8.7 billion FY '77 federal budget for such activity, a 150 percent increase in that category over the past ten years. The principal activities are energy, health, and basic research. This $8.7 billion sum is fast approaching what private sources themselves devote to Research and Development. The federal funds are even more influential, since they tend to address the longer term while industry funds address largely the shorter lead-time work. Thus the federal work will tend to establish the platform from which the world of the future will spring.

Why am I hopeful about this situation? Government is going to play a role; it won't be turned off. Can it play that role without stifling the spontaneity of the cohort of diverse contributors who have traditionally determined the future through their thousands of personal decisions and personal interests pursued day after day? Much thought should be given to this topic and is being given, but so far the prescriptions center on less direct funding and master-minding by government and more use of indirect funding, through incentives. The use of incentives that point toward general goals without master-minding how those goals will be reached or if they will be reached is promising, but too little explored or experienced for a full evaluation. Despite the tentative nature of incentive proposals so far, the idea of federal incentives, an idea commonly used in the private sector, may well have a role in the future of the innovation chain.

There may be other approaches too—for example, those pointed at reduced regulation by federal agencies and commissions. The hopeful sign is that government and industry alike are beginning to collaborate to augment innovation, at the same time looking for ways of preserving the individual and institutional freedoms that have traditionally been the bedrock of the diversity that is a unique feature of society in this country.

The subject of the innovation chain is attracting more and more the attention of economists and politicians as an element of international economic policy. Simon Kuznets, winner of the Nobel Prize for economics, has said: "The major capital stock of an industrialized advanced nation is not its physical equipment. It is the body of knowledge amassed from tested findings of empirical science and the capacity and training of its population to use this knowledge effectively." Indeed, statesmen, managers, and politicians are increasingly using technology and know-how as tools in their trades.

The United States Government has science and technology agreements with the Soviet Union, Japan, France, and twenty-five other countries. Under these agreements, there are information exchanges, visits by teams and individuals, and even jointly performed research and development. The cost to the United States is estimated to exceed $50 million a year. In all this activity the diplomatic profits are more important than the technical ones to the sponsoring governments. This viewpoint has a long history, beginning with the idea that the laws of nature are universal, not subject to political boundaries. Thus science and technology have been the bedrock of mutual interest between many nations even when their other vital interests have conflicted. For example, science and technology exchange was the first evidence of a beginning thaw in the Cold War between the West and the Soviet Bloc in the late 1950's and early 1960's. And this exchange has not been eroded despite the fall of détente as an accepted goal.

One can go further and say that there are four principal forces in world affairs outside of military strength. These are natural resources, educated manpower, capital investment, and technology. All are necessary for any nation's development and growth, but technology seems the most pervasive, and the other three factors themselves are technology-dependent. Little wonder that a worldwide tug-of-war is developing between nations over these necessities through natural resource cartels such as OPEC, brain drains, special banks for investment and credit to the poorer sectors of the world, and nontariff barriers to technology import and export.

This same tension is reflected in the evolving rhetoric between the developing and developed nations—currently framed in the so-called North-South dialogues. The demands of the developing world can be summed up as money (for commodities) and free technology. On the international scene, advanced technology provides prestige and freedom of action. International "interdependence" is a widely voiced theme, but nations do not accept interdependence enforced through their technological inferiority.

Reinforcing this technological nationalism is the association between advanced technology and a favorable balance of trade. This is most evident in the value-added economies of Japan, Western Europe, and the United States. These economies depend upon taking raw materials, many of them imported, and adding value by producing sophisticated products. This is a highly technology-dependent activity. The international trade flow illustrates the situation. The United States balance of trade is very favorable in high-technology products—aircraft, computers, communication equipment, drugs and chemicals, and machine tools. Agricultural products are another high-technology export. Such exports bring wealth to a country, and their principal content lies in the technology essential to their high value. This is the source of desire by developing nations for technology. If the most vehement nationalistic policies can be diluted, there is a good chance that developing nations can achieve at least some of their goals. Those countries that live by the strategy of attracting private investment through the market mechanism will secure technology, and they will prosper. The innovation chain is quietly beginning to have a salutary effect on the international scene.

These are not nearly all the hopeful signs I see, but they illustrate the point of this essay—that science and technology coupled effectively to innovation make not only a strong reed but the only reed for society to lean on. Not that all concerns will disappear. If we think deeply about the energy crisis, population growth, and shortages of food, materials, and human resources, we come away with the conviction that there can be no final solutions. Indeed, these problems are often stated so that there can be no final solutions. We can see, however, that scribbles and experiments will continue to change the world. Those changes will create new worlds for us to live in, worlds in which the insoluble problems will be submerged. Of course, they will reappear with different intensities in different forms and with different names. But given the wise application of human intelligence sustained over decades, these problems will not overcome us either. In this continuing transformation, science and technology, adequately coupled to needs, individual as well as collective, are our best resource for preserving the touchstone of American society—freedom through diversity and pluralism.

6. TECHNOLOGY AND
THE QUALITY OF LIFE

William D. Carey

*William D. Carey is Executive Director of the American Associa-
tion for the Advancement of Science, Washington, D.C. From
1942 until 1969, Mr. Carey held positions with the Bureau of
the Budget, where he was the Bureau's principal spokesman on
matters of science and technology, and served in the Executive
Office of the President of the United States. He was a Vice
President with Arthur D. Little, Inc., from 1969 until assum-
ing his present post in 1975. He has written widely and is one of
the world's acknowledged authorities on science and technology
policy.*

THE OPENING LINE from *Scaramouche* comes to mind: "He
was born with the gift of laughter and a sense that the world was
mad." Sabatini was obviously describing someone born before
his time with gifts that would be handy in this age of distemper
—a sense of humor and a saving perspective toward one's fellow
men and what they imagine they are up to.

I have often wished that in preparing young people for life,
we tried harder to equip them with both humor and perspective
—but I suppose we would louse that up, too. As I view the performance of managers and decision-makers, in government and
in business, neither humor nor perspective receives enough scope,
though they would be good antidotes to the pretentiousness that
afflicts most managerial style. The humorless pragmatist is very
good at avoiding small mistakes, but he has a fine talent for the

Mr. William D. Carey.

bigger ones. And surely, if there is a reason for us to take note of the 75th year of the Tuck School, as well as the bicentennials of Adam Smith and American independence, it is to reexamine their meanings and come away with fresh perspectives.

Those who know me are aware that I am a hopeless biblio-holic—I crave books of any description. I mention this because the other night, for some reason, I remembered the excitement I felt at my first reading, more than thirty years ago, in Samuel

Eliot Morison's *Admiral of the Ocean Sea,* the story of Columbus'
voyages of discovery. So I took it from the shelf and began to
browse. (I did not then know, coincidentally, that it was the last
weekend of Morison's wonderfully full life.) And in the prologue
of that book the uses of perspective struck me again, because he
was writing about the cultural and philosophical environment of
Columbus' own times. Morison did it by quoting from the *Nuremberg Chronicle* of July 14, 1493, a chronicle which claims mod-
estly that it contains "the events most worthy of notice from
the beginning of the world to the calamity of our time." That
time, and that calamity, of course, was the closing decade of the
fifteenth century. As Morison put it,

*Lest any reader feel an unjustified optimism, the Nuremberg
chroniclers place 1493 in the Sixth or Penultimate Age of the
world, leaving just six blank pages to record events from the
date of printing to the Day of Judgment. Then begins a proph-
ecy of the Seventh and final Age—and quoting from the Chronicle—"in comparison with which our age, in which iniquity and
evil have increased to the highest pitch, may be regarded as
happy and almost golden." Only the wicked will prosper, good
men will fall into contempt and penury; there will be no faith,
no law, no justice, no humanity, no shame, and no truth.*

But, Morison says, even as the chroniclers of Nuremberg were
scripting that awful future, a Spanish caravel named *Nina* was
scudding before a winter gale into Lisbon with news of a discovery that was to give old Europe another chance.

    This, of course, puts forecasting into the right perspective.
In some ways, it seems to me that the heirs of the Nuremberg
chroniclers are still scribbling, still predicting the Seventh and
last age of man, still discounting the possibilities of thought,
discovery, and enterprise for giving tired and troubled institutions another chance. It is not social criticism to which I object,
because that has its uses in every age, and it reminds us that we

have choices. It is another thing when criticism creates a national mind set which makes us believe that our options have all been foreclosed by our failures. We would not be the first great nation to be victimized by its own myths. A people that believes it will not get another chance is a people that bears very careful watching.

The great public trial of American technology, now in full flower, is a case in point. There is a moral judgment in the air, and on balance it is adverse to technological achievement. The thrust of this moral judgment is explicit. It says that an incompatibility exists between technology and the quality of life; that man's inherent freedoms and prospects are retreating in the face of technological holocaust. The indictment is not without its bill of particulars: our fascination with weapons technology, our use of defoliants on a backward people, the threatened degradation of the biosphere by aviation technology, the killing of the wetlands by development and pollution, the infringement of privacy by telecommunications technology, the implicit threats of nuclear power technology, and more. It suffices. It is a bill of particulars and then some, and the moral judgment is passed swiftly.

Yet the morality is ambivalent. Along come demands for full employment, for increased productivity, for independence in energy and materials, for product reliability and safety, for technology transfer to third-world countries, for a favorable United States balance of international payments, for electronic banking, for better information systems—and there is hardly a pause in the Congress as the defense appropriations bill rolls on to enactment. Well, where does the moral issue begin and end? Apparently, it all depends. Miles's Law applies: Where one stands depends on where one sits.

But I think this much is clear: technology cannot prosper long in the United States under a moral cloud. The present signs are not exactly optimistic—a visible decline in technological vitality and risk-taking, a proliferation of government regulation, widespread hedging against uncertainty, few new formations of small innovative firms, industry preoccupation with defensive research and development, and very long lead times from innovation to marketing. An adverse moral judgment may not be to blame for all these signs, but it is certainly part of the problem.

How a society views itself is partly at issue, of course, and it takes us right back to the need for some perspective. In a recent column in the *Washington Post,* Henry Owen quoted Burkhardt and Acton to the effect that a culture rooted in pragmatism would be vulnerable to great pressures and temptations. Now I accept that in principle, and I think that as a pragmatic culture we are not immune to the warning. But I am prepared to argue that the American culture, over its brief history, has been conspicuous for its altruism and for an astonishing moral innocence. At the same time, it has not yielded very often to pressures and temptations—and when it has, it has usually been caught and chastised.

I think that, on the whole, the evidence for what I have called altruism is both strong and consistent, all the way from treaty obligations, which have been a matter of embarrassment, to a deeply centered antipathy toward economic and political corruption, to a belief in the rule of law, a passion for universal education, a healthy dislike of obtrusive power in any form, and faith in economic competition. To be sure, the pragmatism is there, too. If it were not, there would be little excellence and a lot of mediocrity. Pragmatism is no basis for declaring a calamity; and if we had any less of it, there would be neither the resources nor the enterprise to reach the qualitative goals that make for a humane society. It is what makes such choices possible. The moral problem is that some choices are better than others, but I know of neither a moral law nor a public law that can keep us from making mistakes, though we seem to behave as though the opposite were true. The result is that we are so complicating our decision-making that an administered society is gradually coming to pass, and we will get it because it seems that we want it.

In this vein, I think of a woman who lives in Princeton and runs an impoverished public interest center out of her house. Her name is Hazel Henderson, and not long ago she caught my attention with an article on the "Entropy State." The Entropy State, in her terms, is a society where complexity is carried to such lengths that the society slowly winds down of its own weight, with all its forces and counterforces checked and balanced in a state of equilibrium. How near are we to the Entropy State? Ask yourselves, as you listen to part of her argument.

Because advanced industrial societies develop such unmanageable complexity, they naturally generate a bewildering increase in unanticipated social costs: in human maladjustment, community disruption, and environmental depletion... The costs of cleaning up the mess and caring for the human casualties of unplanned technology—the dropouts, the unskilled, the addicts, or those who just cannot cope with the maze of urban life or deal with Big Brother bureaucracies—mounts ever higher. The proportion of GNP that must be spent in mediating conflicts, controlling crime, protecting consumers and the environment, providing ever more comprehensive bureaucratic coordination, and generally trying to maintain social homeostasis begins to grow exponentially. New levels of expenditure to maintain this social homeostasis are augured daily, as in the recent calls for new legislation to provide government compensation for crime victims and assist those who succumb to chronic debt.

There you have one perspective on what is going on, and there is enough to it to be troubling. In a long life in government I learned that the itch to pass new corrective laws and erect new administrative procedures is an itch that never subsides, no matter how many legislative powders and poultices come on the market. Entropy advances while confidence recedes, and the "fed up with government" mentality spreads and cultivates what becomes the greatest of dangers for a democratic society: it brings the demagogue out of the shadows and makes him plausible.

But to question the growth of government is one thing, while painting government as a conspiracy on the Potomac is another. I sense that an antigovernment psychology is sweeping the land. At the risk of being a party spoiler, I should like to make a point or two.

I am weary of hearing government kicked around by opportunistic politicians and self-appointed wise men. We went through all this in the 1950's, and it moved a new President to ask that we resolve to make the public service a proud and lively career. I want to tell you that mine *was* proud, and it *was* lively. And if we run the public service down, if we hound it, if we show only contempt for it, then we will break its heart and its spirit, and I call that wrong. We will get third-rate public service if our expectations for it are third rate. We will drive off the best of our young people from public service as a career, and we will end with what we deserve.

I can tell you that public management is a hard and exacting profession, that it is no less a field of advanced management than one finds in the best of the business world; that coping with uncertainty is no small part of it; and that choices at the margin are no easier in that environment than elsewhere. So when we talk so glibly about simplifying government and stripping off its trappings, I am here to say that this is nonsense. This isn't the nineteenth century. The scale is entirely different, the risks are enormous, the response times shorter, the demands greater, and the resources scarcer.

I want to weep at the shallowness of the presidential contest of the bicentennial year, which ought to have been a year of intense and profound debate about the uses of power and responsibility, instead of what was served up. I see not a shred of great-

ness in the candidates, not a sign of vision. Yet, we are worship-
ing those political ancestors: Franklin, Jefferson, Adams,
Hamilton—who did have greatness, and who did have vision, and
because of it they made a difference. Instead, we seem to have
to choose among men who know all that they are against but
nothing that they are for.

We had better try to understand that the policies and the
decision-making of government will have to be very good if we
are to get through this century in an interdependent world,
because we no longer hold all the high cards and we are very
vulnerable. Government and the public service are not the whole
answer but they are part of it, and instead of sneering at government and demeaning it, we ought to look to its strength, its
expectations, its legitimacy, and its pride of service. These things
I believe very deeply.

I tend to take Hazel Henderson's point that unplanned
technology is a factor contributing to the Entropy State, though
I think that the plot is thicker than that. There is a case against
mindless technological growth, and against the idea that in any
confrontation with the quality of life technology must come out
on top.

I believe that here the moral question does arise, and that if
technological initiative is not to be regulated into the ground by
government or condemned to endless litigation, we will have to
look for some alternative passage, however narrow, that leads to
daylight. I think it must take the form of a qualitative assessment
of major innovations at that stage of decision-making in the firm
when the commitment to invest heavily in development and
market preparation has to be made. It should be a process that
is built into the behavior of the firm as a good corporate citizen.
I know no reason why technology assessment has to be reserved
for people in government who wear white hats and are far removed from the realities of market experience. And I suggest
this with every confidence that otherwise a day will come when

some kinetic member of Congress puts in a bill based on the interstate commerce power and the general welfare clause imposing a technology assessment system on private industry with the full menu of rules, regulations, reports, enforcers, civil penalties, and citizen participation. Do not underestimate the Entropy State.

The issue of technological morality as it concerns the humane society is the offspring of a somewhat different ethic, which surfaced roughly a decade ago. It was the very complex matter of accountability, and it was first raised in an articulate way by Alan Pifer of the Carnegie Foundation in connection with what he christened the "quasi-nongovernmental organization," referring to the undefined class of enterprises which had grown up for public interest reasons without being unambiguously in either the purely private or purely public sector. And this profoundly difficult question of the limits of accountability and independence had a great deal to do with the recognition that society had indeed become so complex, the governmental and economic structures so huge, and big decisions so irreversible that the citizen was left with almost no role or power to affect his environment and his future. So we began to question the system, to ask who, if anyone, was in fact accountable, and what the properties of accountability consisted of. This had very little to do with technology itself, though in time technology was to draw much of the heat, but in the main the questions ran to the search for preventive constraints on the irresponsible use of power against the common interest—as that interest came to be defined in environmental policy terms, then in privacy protection laws, then in limitations on presidential power, in the appearance of the idea of technology assessment, then in the fields of consumer protection and credit disclosure, and lastly in the area of rules of campaign financing. Whether all this, or some part of it, explains the extraordinary refusal of so many senators and congressmen to stand for reelection even from safe seats, I cannot say. But I am tempted to wonder. The point is that this was the tidal wave of demand for more explicit accountability, and it begat a flood of moral questioning which crested with the debacles of Vietnam, the energy crisis, and the fall of the President. It brought with it a collapse in human institutions and value systems, and its course is not yet run. As with the Nuremberg chroniclers, a sense of calamity swept the land, and as in 1493, it seemed that one could hear and see a world of no faith, no law, no humanity, and no truth. We were never more vulnerable, never closer to a total breakdown of perspective, never so far from laughter.

Has it run its course? I think of an article in the *New York Times Sunday Magazine* a few months back, by a university professor of humanistic studies, entitled "Knowledge Dethroned." Its thrust was an explanation of why it is that scientists and scholars have fallen from grace. The thesis was that the public has grown disenchanged with the postwar promises of learning and that a sense of the failures of knowledge lies upon the land. It is a proposition that we should examine very carefully, for if it is correct, the whole house of learning is in a lot of trouble. When public opinion comes to believe that knowledge is a mixture of arrogance and fraud, trust is withdrawn from learning and know-nothingism rises again. Perhaps, here today in this center of learning and thought, these ideas have the same ring of the absurd as the works of the overwrought chroniclers of Nuremberg. But we have seen, and continue to see, a rising disenchantment with the search for new knowledge. We see it in the mauling of the National Science Foundation at the hands of some members of Congress. The shaming of science has become profitable and rewarding politics. Research projects with unusual titles and objectives are ambushed and paraded in the streets to a drumfire of ridicule and intimidation, and it is not much exaggeration to say that social science and behavioral research in the United States are coming under political siege. The danger is not that science will cease, but that it will be forced by the power of government financial support to bend to a political standard of acceptance. When that happens, our science will become cheapened and humiliated, and there is no good in that. Toynbee, if I remember rightly, tallied up not one but twenty dark periods in man's history, and it is not hard to see how narrow is the passage through which we must find our way.

As a people capable of perspective, our problem is to resist being so traumatized by crisis, doubt, and guilt that we are frozen into immobility and indecision. Such a people will not build, they will only burrow. We have already been partially numbed by the nightmares of the limits to growth, future shock, the failures of knowledge, and the psychology of calamity. Bit by bit, we are diminished. Nobody rises to remind us that of all of the ages of man, ours is the most creative, the most abundant, the most literate, the most vital. If it is also the most complex, interdependent, and vulnerable, then knowledge and its right uses—touched by a capacity for reverence—must get us through.

If we are running through the world's resources, if we are too slow in closing the gap between advanced and developing countries, if we are pouring stupefying amounts of money into weapons while we talk peace, if we are endangering our natural environment, if we are encroaching on personal privacy—the answers lie less in quarantining technology than in reason and responsibility in its uses. This assumption, that intelligent and moral growth will see us through, seems to run through the new report by the Hudson Institute—"The Next 200 Years"—which argues that the gap between rich and poor nations is itself the strongest force for closing that gap without the help of uprisings or wars. And the Institute's forecast for the year 2176—which will be the 275 anniversary of the Tuck School and the quadricentennial of Adam Smith—is that gross world product will go from its present $5 trillion level to $300 trillion. That is quite a leap from the bell-tolling of the Club of Rome, and it says something about comparative perspectives. We don't know, of course, whether Herman Kahn's world of 2176 will be wiser in managing a $300 trillion economy than we were with our puny $5 trillion one. What will be the quality of life in such a world? Will it value music, art, thought, beauty, and laughter? Will the unit of society be the nation, the continent, or the hemisphere? Will the scale permit democracy, or require autarchy? One comes back to the question put 100 years ago by Thomas Huxley at the close of his first visit to the United States.

To an Englishman landing upon your shores for the first time, seeing your enormous wealth, there is something sublime in the vista of the future. Do not suppose that I am pandering to what is commonly understood by national pride. I cannot say that I am in the slightest degree impressed by your bigness, or your material resources, as such. Size is not grandeur, and territory does not make a nation. The great question, about which hangs a true sublimity, and the terror of overhanging fate, is: What are you going to do with all these things? What is to be the end of which these are the means?

I have little patience with the indiscriminating indictment of technology as the chief enemy of the quality of life. Technology has done less harm to civilized existence than have cultural prejudice and discrimination, lazy education, compulsive consumption, and the devaluation of excellence and achievement as personal goals. I think that technology served man well earlier this month when a team of Johns Hopkins surgeons replaced the cancerous part of an eleven-year-old boy's leg, using telescopic and surgical microscopes during a fourteen-hour operation, rather than having to amputate. I suggest that something good happened to the quality of life at the recent AAAS meeting in Boston when I saw a paraplegic scientist get around in a special wheelchair which he could command and control by activating an electronic mechanism with the tip of his nose. I suggest that blacks and other minorities in the labor force have only one real alternative to chronic unemployment and the humiliations of the welfare system, and it is the economic growth which creates work opportunities, a growth that depends on technological initiatives and risk-taking. I feel that the LANSAT satellite and its remote-sensing capacities for mapping natural resources will accelerate the progress of poor races and nations. I suggest that future technologies of laser fusion and bioconversion will capture from the seas and the sun the energy to meet our need. It isn't sufficient to see only technology's dark side. There is light, and hope, and wonder in this power that man has come to know.

CLOSING REMARKS

John W. Hennessey, Jr.

I FEEL very fortunate indeed to be sitting in the pilothouse of
the good ship Amos Tuck School on this special anniversary
occasion, and especially at this banquet tonight. After nineteen
years on board, I have developed great respect and affection for
this institution and what it represents. I thank you all for the
kind remarks you have made about Tuck School—past, present,
and future—in its questful adventure on the high seas of collegiate education. And you were more than kind to speak some
phrases, generous indeed, about my deanship as one focus for
your thoughts about the School and its adventure.

Tonight we look back seventy-five years, to 1900 and 1901
—when the Century of Steam ended and the Century of Electric-
ity began, when J. P. Morgan organized U.S. Steel, when Nietzsche, Verdi, and Queen Victoria died, when Picasso began his
blue period, and when Freud wrote *Interpretation of Dreams*.

Inside this larger context, the history of the founding of
Tuck School makes fascinating reading. There is no doubt that
the School owes its creation principally to two people. They
were both essential to the success of the invention. I refer, as
you know, to Dr. William Jewett Tucker, Dartmouth's ninth
president (1893–1907) and his erstwhile Dartmouth roommate
from the Class of 1862, Edward Tuck, who named this School
for his father Amos.

Dr. Tucker first articulated in 1896, as far as we can tell,
his concern that there had been a substantial growth in interest
among Dartmouth graduates in business careers. Paralleling the
great growth of commercial enterprise in America and the new

Dr. John W. Hennessey, Jr.

need for executives or managers, by 1896 20 percent of Dartmouth's graduates were seeking commercial and financial careers,
compared with 2 percent in 1810. Dr. Tucker strongly felt the
social value of creating a preparation for business *leadership*
which would profit from the models used by Dartmouth in
medicine and engineering. And he especially valued the thought
that Dartmouth should "bridge the gap between the liberal college and the world of affairs." He said, "It was a confession of
the inutility or narrowness of a liberal education, for the colleges
to leave their graduates in a helpless attitude before their new

Richard West, John Hennessey, and Arthur Upgren, Respectively the Sixth, Fifth, and Third Deans of the Tuck School.

responsibilities, or to commit them to the fortune of their personal initiative."

As Russell Larmon wrote in 1932, it was noteworthy that a spiritual and intellectual leader like Dr. Tucker should have taken this new step, and that it should have been so quickly and heartily endorsed by Edward Tuck, a man of high cultural interest and tastes, living in Paris. Both men felt the "bridge" I referred to was a proper one; that Tuck School should build on the unorganized cultural interests and values of undergraduate years. Tuck was to be a place to blend ideals and values and sympathies effectively, raising business to the dignity of a profession—involving knowledge, skill, and the acceptance of obligation to one's fellows.

It is gratifying to read of Dr. Tucker's satisfaction with the results he saw in Tuck School. Shortly before his retirement, he

wrote to Edward Tuck, "I find that among the different influ-
ences which are at work to build up the College, none is more
marked, at present, than the Tuck School idea."

Mr. Tuck, on his own initiative, became the first person of
means to contribute significant funds to the new and rebuilt
Dartmouth, before there was any solicitation of any sort on the
part of the College. His gifts were not only unsolicited, they
were a great surprise.

The history of Mr. Tuck's thirty-eight years of unparalleled
philanthropy is amazing to read. His correspondence with Presidents Tucker, Nichols, and Hopkins is a chronicle of the most
thoughtful anticipation of the best interests of the College,
ranging from faculty salaries to the President's home and from
Tuck Drive to all of the buildings which Tuck School occupied
for its first sixty-eight years, starting with the handsome edifice
now called McNutt, which was Tuck Hall for twenty-six years
and built for the sum of $85,000! In all he gave the College more
than $4,500,000, which still stands as the record.

Mr. Tuck was a remarkable man. A millionaire at a young
age, he lived nearly all of his adult years in Paris and died there
in 1938 at the age of 95. From a great array of notable facts
about the man and about his wife, Julia Stell, it is evident that
the French nation held them in especial esteem. From an article
by Horatio Krans we know that Mr. Tuck was an admirer "and
an assiduous reader of Benjamin Franklin." They were kindred
spirits in several ways, including their affection for France.
Common to both was "a ceaseless flow of humor, a humor not
without its audacities." Engraved on Mr. Tuck's monument in
the cemetery of St. Germain is a Franklin quotation prized by
Tuck:

*The years roll by and the last will come, when I would rather
have it said, "He lived usefully" than "He died rich."*

The correspondence between close friends Tuck and Tucker
is steady and fulsome. I was surprised at the social technology of

their reluctance ever to use first names. (It was always "My dear Tuck or Tucker" and the signature was always full names.) Yet the letters were intimate and most spirited. At times Edward Tuck became a bit avuncular, I note. He was wont to give advice on small things, although he never interfered with policy (even when he and President Tucker saw national events rather differently). Among Mr. Tuck's bits of advice was a sentence in the August 29, 1901, letter: "I hear from time to time complaints of the discreditable carriage accommodation from the station to the town, and of the poor hotel in Hanover." (I'd like to think Mr. Tuck rests in peace knowing we have indeed taken care of *one* of those problems.) The only piece of persistent advice I am glad the Tuck faculty did not adopt was to give RR management such a central place that indeed the School might have become the Tuck School of Railroading and Finance. On the other hand, had Tuck School become a fountain of leadership for America's railroads, who knows in what splendid comfort we might have been able to travel in America today!

Often the Tuck and Tucker letters were in longhand. Indeed, President Tucker had no secretary until 1895 or 1896. When he became President in May 1893 there was "no secretary, no typist, no typewriter, no telephone," according to historians Leavens and Lord. "The one full-time administrator was the President." He personally answered in longhand all inquiries from applicants.

As a sidelight, I find it relevant that between 1893 and 1900 Dr. Tucker often spoke of changes in the College presidency—the new need he saw for executive management in addition to intellectual and spiritual leadership. I really think these thoughts were harmonic with his receptivity to the founding of Tuck School.

The establishment of the School was the creation of a model—and by 1976 I can testify that MBA programs have proliferated almost as if there were an assembly line producing them. The model has been a success! There have been three main eras of development, and Tuck has played an important role in each.

Until 1916 business schools featured theory from basic disciplines and courses in "how to do it." From 1917 to 1946 they added lots of rich, descriptive material, an energetic chronicling of economic institutions and the work of people in them. From 1946 on, the added emphasis has been analytical.

I spoke a moment ago of growth. Despite the Tuck model, the greatest proliferation of business education has been at the undergraduate level. As recently as 1959, 90 percent of the degrees given in the field were baccalaureate, but by 1969 18 percent of the degrees were Master's, and that figure is higher today. In the last decade it is clear that the quickened pace of change, deepened impact of complexity, and other factors have pressed on the academic work of business schools on all sides and produced a new sophistication and toughness, a new rigor in business education—most evident in the privileged, leading schools.

This has meant a retreat from vocationalism in its more vulgar form, a move from domination by the business profession toward more governance by the academy (with strong advisory boards—like our Overseers), less the image of West Points of capitalism, now an old-fashioned metaphor.

In addition, the modern business school increasingly has its own subject matter: decision-making, administration, other analytics. More than applied economics, management science has a new status (and so has the art of management in our organized society).

Business schools have developed the environmental field better than any other professional area. I mean not just the ecological, but, more enduringly, the economic, political, and social environment of enterprise. Our Professor Wayne Broehl has been a leader in two decades of consciousness-raising, anticipating the modern critique of the corporation in its external relations.

Today's challenge to the School of Management is a robust

one, worthy of the *best* the university can bring to it. The business school carries a stewardship to aid its students to cope responsibly and effectively with an unknowable future and to be life-long learners at a time of informational explosion, dazzling communication overload, and the heightened feeling of consequentiality.

Students in a modern management school have a right to expect to learn about the analysis of and optimal responses to the widest range of complex, purposive, organizational phenomena—private and public, profit and not-for-profit, producing goods and producing services, materialistic and humanistic. As we have seen in our day and a half, there are mind-boggling questions of effectiveness-efficiency for all organizations at a time of attenuated growth, moderated optimism, and the obvious interdependence among all resources. As the colloquia of yesterday and today have illustrated, there *are* great and abiding issues of the means and ends of modern existence which find their most accessible expression in economics, in work in organizations, and in management.

These issues have a proper home in the MBA curriculum. They also supply the energy and focus for management school research, pushing back the darkness both in basic disciplines and in the high intellectual calling of fruitful, wise applications, in a real world and real time context, and in the wider public interest.

One of the most interesting demands on the business school is that it deals with modern uncertainty and complexity, and these forces have great human implications. Of course decision-making thrives amidst uncertainty. And I would reject as a mere wisecrack *Business Week's* use of the phrase "MBA syndrome," which Bill Carey mentioned.

Bertrand Russell said, "The rise to authority is often achieved by those who feel the strongest certainty on matters on which doubt is the only rational attitude." This is only one of the many parodoxes of the life of action. Another is that

ends become means, and means, ends. Small wonder some of the
abiding concerns about organizational life have to do with attach-
ing accountability to power, human rights to governance, and
wisdom to justice. These profound questions in western life
today require a collaboration of the management scholar and
the moral philosopher. Forgive me the Apostrophe, but "Adam
Smith where are you when we need you!" In rediscovering the
real Adam Smith this year, as our panelists have attested, we see
he was one of the most profound moral philosophers of western
civilization.

The lingering question of two centuries of productive ma-
terialism is: where does man fit? Of what consequence is the
belief that man is an end, infinitely valuable and not to be
treated as means? Is this concern a precious pietism or is it a
light with which to find our way out of the twentieth century?
And what is the goal of human existence? Is it useful to say it is
material prosperity, power, or even freedom? A surprising part
of Solzhenitsyn's dialectic, to me, is his point that liberty is a
means, *not* an end! Or are these all means to the higher end of
enhancing the human spirit? And how do formal organizations
fit in such rhetoric and the reality it represents? William Carey
inspired us to look that question in the eye when he referred to
"a humane society." We asked our speakers about the future. I
think their best advice to us was, stay loose and maintain your
sense of humor, perspective, and integrity. Two presidential
election years from now comes 1984. Is George Orwell's fantas-
tic prediction waiting for us?

Meanwhile, back in the corporation what signs does one
see? I think there are important stirrings—reaction to the giant-
ism that dwarfs humans and the specialization which corrupts
humaneness, and our speakers pointed to some of these and
quoted Adam Smith on urging them. A combination of the
public requirement for various new accountabilities, plus a re-
visionist attitude toward boards of directors, the rights of groups

previously on the periphery of power (women and minorities)—
all of this and other experiments in humanistic decision-making
may lead to new discontinuities in Western life. I am optimistic
that the results, at least in the short-run, will be significant im-
provements in organizational service to human values.

As 1975–76 draws to a close, Tuck School concludes its
diamond anniversary, a special time of celebrating its origins and
assessing its contributions to the prosperity in America of the
idea of management education at the Master's level. It is a moment to salute, with pride, the people who have made Tuck
School the vital institution it is—the alumni and faculty most
especially. As I leave the dean post I feel a very special debt to
those who preceded me: Messrs. Person and Dixon; William Gray,
who first carried the title Dean and served so productively for
eighteen years; Herluf Olsen, 1937 to 1952, who saw the School
through World War II and the rebuilding which followed; Arthur
Upgren (1953 to 1957), who laid the basic policies for the important diversification of the student body; and Karl Hill, Dean
from 1957 to 1968, who developed the momentum of our
modern progress. The result is a School of distinction among its
peers, poised on a cheerful and positive pivot in its history. *And
proud to be part of the modern Dartmouth.*

This seems a natural point at which to stride with confidence from one era to another. Tuck, like Dartmouth, has moved
into the national limelight as a distinctive institution of sound
resources and high selectivity. Its remarkably singular concentra-
tion on the MBA as its only degree program sets it in marked
contrast to all the other 190 accredited collegiate business
schools in the country and gives it an obvious invitation to be
the best of the lot. With its high tuition and enviably small size,
it must be special—to the extent of serving not only as a source
of future leaders but also as a pilot plant in which tomorrow's
MBA model is built and tested. One might say the same of the
School's well developed Executive Program, already a well-

tested model of continued learning, thanks to Professor Kenneth Davis.

The challenge to Tuck as it enters its fourth quarter of a century is to nurture executive leadership in new ways, consistent with prescient predictions about the life that managers will lead in the 1980's and 1990's. Increasingly, the consumers of Tuck's MBA education—students and employers alike—will expect Tuck to be venturesome in its vision of the future and in its investments in ways of understanding and managing the process of change itself. This is true not only for business, but also for other kinds of organizations—dependent on managerial wisdom and skill. There is much to respect and even cherish in the accumulated wisdom of seventy-five years. But in the pleasant afterglow of an anniversary celebration, one has a rare opportunity not only to honor heritage but also to address the future anew—and to think of values.

Richard West's arrival as Tuck's sixth dean augurs admirably well for Tuck School. In the first place, what a boost to Tuck that a candidate from the very top of the selection list was persuaded to accept the job! Nothing could corroborate so aptly our growing sense of both achievement and promise in the School. I want to emphasize his modernity, his unencumbered freshness. I think the School has found just the right person to suit the moment and to sharpen Tuck's focus on the future. In Frederick Webster, Dean West has selected a teammate Associate Dean who will fill the job with unusual commitment, talent, and energy—carrying on in the Paganucci tradition. And may I add my personal pleasure that Paul Paganucci will stay on this campus —and thus remain a pillar in the Tuck community.

May I conclude on a personal note. As I take up the attractive duties of Charles Henry Jones Third Century Professor of the Management of Man, I am aware that transmuted deans are apt to be nervous creatures when loosed among veteran teacher/ scholars. No doubt that is why I am permitted to begin my

Jones Chair stewardship with a sabbatical leave. With a year of contemplative preparation for intensive professing, I expect gradually to learn to do without the firebells of administrative urgencies, the roaring waterfall of information flows, the whistling winds of new external exigencies, or the special smell of ambiguity and uncertainty which those winds often leave behind.

While I may be removed from the natural arena of these phenomena, I will not be far away. I will be studying just those managerial metaphors with whatever social science tools and insights seem useful. They are the very stuff good case studies in the management of man are made of. And will I not be envied the hope that my deaning will increase my chances of evoking fruitful hypotheses for research on managerial behavior, with only a modicum of pedantry. If for the dean the proper injunction is, "Don't just sit there, do something," to the Professor of Management there is better wisdom in "Don't just do something, sit there." I intend to try to obey the least trite and most flattering interpretation of that invitation back to the faculty.

Thank you, one and all, for helping to make this anniversary celebration such an intellectually stimulating experience and such a pleasant and valued Tuck-family affair!